THE JOY OF DISCOVERY

IN BIBLE STUDY

●

Revised Edition

●

OLETTA WALD

AUGSBURG PUBLISHING HOUSE
MINNEAPOLIS, MINNESOTA

THE JOY OF DISCOVERY IN BIBLE STUDY

Revised edition copyright © 1975 by Augsburg Publishing House

Library of Congress Catalog Card No. 75-22710

International Standard Book No. 0-8066-1513-3

Scripture quotations unless otherwise noted are from the Revised Standard Version of the Bible, copyright 1946, 1952, and 1971 by the Division of Christian Education of the National Council of Churches.

Scripture quotations from Today's English Version (TEV), copyright 1966 by American Bible Society, are used by permission.

Manufactured in the United States of America

CONTENTS

INTRODUCTION

This book is a revised edition of my book, *The Joy of Discovery.* I wrote the first edition soon after I attended the former Biblical Seminary in New York, where I was introduced to what is called *inductive Bible study.* In this book, I shall call the process *discovery Bible study.* While this revised edition contains the same basic principles described in the first edition, I have changed the format and rearranged the material. The focus now is only on Bible *study.* The section on Bible *teaching* has been omitted. This will be included in a companion book. The purpose of this book is to involve you in Bible study skills which will enable you to experience the joy that can be yours as you learn to become a discoverer of the truths in the Bible.

A "Flounderer" in Bible Study

I had been a student of the Bible several years before I learned how to become a discoverer on my own. I could follow the suggestions of others and answer the questions they asked, but I floundered when I tried to launch out for myself. I did not know where to start or what to do. The treasures of the Bible seemed locked behind abstract words. I always had to depend on someone else to open the door.

Learning the Secret

While a student at the former Biblical Seminary in New York, I was taught how to explore the truths of the Bible in a methodical and systematic way. I learned some steps to take when studying a passage. I found that it was like working a combination lock. When I followed the steps, the Word opened up to me. I felt free. I realized that I was no longer dependent on others to gain insights into Scripture. I had become a discoverer. In a new way, Bible study had become more meaningful and personal. Most of all it was deeply satisfying to know how to discover the truths in God's Word. I had experienced *the joy of discovery* in Bible study!

Sharing My Discoveries with Others

My new discoveries were too good to keep to myself. I began to teach the skills which I had learned to my students at the Lutheran Bible Institute and to lay persons in congregations. I found that whenever people would conscientiously apply the principles and follow the steps they too became discoverers and experienced greater joy in their study. I felt the need for a resource which would help them in their study; therefore, I wrote *The Joy of Discovery*. But I wrote the book mainly for students in colleges and seminaries. It was prepared to be a textbook in an academic situation.

Need for Revision

Since the writing of the first edition of *The Joy of Discovery* I have been involved in teaching the skills in many situations, both to students in colleges and to lay persons in congregations. Through these many experiences, I began to realize the necessity of revising the book to better meet the needs of those who were using it.

NEED FOR INTRODUCING THE SKILLS GRADUALLY: I have found that it is very important to introduce the skills in discovery Bible study slowly and gradually. If persons were introduced to too many skills at one time or spent too little time on each skill, they became frustrated and discouraged. They were apt to think that the process was too difficult for them and reject the validity of the skills.

NEED FOR SATISFACTION: I found that persons needed to have a measure of satisfaction as they learned each skill. When learning a skill, there is always some frustration in the beginning. But in the process, persons have to experience enough satisfaction to want to continue the learning of the skill. They are not satisfied with the assurance that some day they will find value in what they are learning. They have to see some value in each step of the process.

NEED FOR RECOGNIZING VARIED ABILITIES: Reactions to these discovery skills will vary with people. The degree to which persons become involved in the skills will vary with interests and background, but all can find a measure of satisfaction in the process.

Pattern for This Revision

I have tried to meet these needs in the way I have patterned this book. I am trying to introduce the skills from the easiest to the more complex, beginning with the very simplest and gradually introducing the more difficult ones. The book is divided into two phases: Phase One—The Discovering Phase, chapters 1-6; Phase Two—The Expanding Phase, chapters 7-14. If you are interested in learning the basics in Bible study, you might find Phase One enough for you. But if you are interested in learning how to go more deeply into Bible study, you will want to continue in Phase Two. The hope is that through this pattern, the skills will be introduced gradually enough for you to grasp the process, yet challenging enough to encourage you to continue the study.

My Indebtedness

The methods presented in this book are not new. They have been advocated by biblical scholars down through the years. One of the greatest exponents of methodical Bible study was the late Dr. Wilbur W. White, the founder of the Biblical Seminary in New York, now called the New York Seminary. Charles R. Eberhardt said of him:

> He vowed that as a teacher he would assist the students not only to learn but pre-eminently to learn *how* he learns. The student must be "taught to believe that he is to be throughout life an independent, yet humble, investigator of truth as it presents itself in living form in the literature of Scripture and to find in the Christ its highest and complete personal manifestation."
>
> He wanted his students to be able to go "anywhere with a Bible and an unabridged dictionary" and with these make themselves ready for classroom and the pulpit.

These principles which Dr. White set forth have been proclaimed by his successors at the Seminary and by its countless graduates in all parts of the world. These principles are the background for this booklet.

I am indebted to the many fine teachers at the Biblical Seminary who taught me the methodical principles of Bible study, but in a special way to Professor Robert Traina whose book *Methodical Bible Study* is the basis for this manual. I am grateful to Mr. Traina for permission to use his book as a basis. I urge those who desire a more comprehensive study of methods to read Professor Traina's book. His is the textbook; mine is more of a workbook applying the principles he sets forth.

My Hope

The purpose of this book is to help you become a discoverer in Bible study and experience joy in the process. Most of the chapters contain two aspects of the study: 1) information about the discovery skills and 2) practices which will help you develop the skills. You will learn very little unless you *practice* the suggested skills. They are the most important aspect of the book. Since the purpose of this resource is to teach you *how* to study, do not be too concerned about your results, that is whether you are right or wrong in what you are doing. If you faithfully practice some of the skills, no matter how inadequate you feel, you will soon realize that you are learning to *discover* some of the truths in a passage. Do not become discouraged in the process. Learning skills does take time. The Lord will increase your capacity to gain deeper insight into the Word as you pray, practice, and persevere. Give him—and yourself—time!

The Joy of Discovery

Bible study can be fun! Maybe that statement startles you. Possibly you have always thought that Bible study should be somber and serious. Maybe you are thinking, "Aren't we studying the book which is inspired by God's Spirit? Shouldn't we approach Bible study in a spirit of humility and seriousness? *Fun is merriment, playful action, a game.* Does this mean that we are to treat Bible study like a playful game?"

By *fun* we do not mean any of these things. We are not speaking about the purpose of Bible study, but the process. It is possible to find the process in Bible study engaging, challenging, and a joy. It is possible to have been involved in a study and afterwards say, "Wow, we had a good time today in our study!" This is the kind of fun we mean—a joyful experience because we were learning how to become discoverers of God's Word and we found the process of discovery a joy!

The Joy of Discovery—a Possibility for All

One of the yearnings of my heart is to enable you to become a discoverer and experience the joy that can be yours in the process. While all Christians agree that the Bible should be studied, many do not find joy in their study. They know very little about the Bible and feel that it is difficult to understand. To them it is a strange book, seemingly too hard or too dull, and they have little inclination to read or study it. This is a tragedy, because Bible study can be a most rewarding, challenging, and exciting study. It can really be fun!

Maybe you are one of those who is saying, "I don't know how to study the Bible. When I read it, I often have difficulty understanding what I read. I haven't found my studying to be a joy. Is it possible for me to learn how to study so that I can become a discoverer?"

The purpose of this book is to enable you to become a discoverer and in the process experience *the joy of discovery.*

As I write, I am well aware that not all of you feel the same way about Bible study. Some of you have been students of the Bible for many years and already know the joy there is in the study. I realize that you can be a variety of ages. Maybe some of you are still in high school. Many of you may be students in a college, Bible school, or seminary. Some of you are leaders, teachers, or missionaries who are guiding others in Bible studies.

I ask myself how I can write a book which will be a challenge to such a variety of people in terms of age, experience and background. I couldn't if it were not that I think you all have one thing in common. You are using this book because you have a deep yearning to learn more about how to study your Bible. My hope and prayer is that you can begin where you are and, through the suggestions in this book, you can develop your potentials as *discoverers*.

Why Become Discoverers?

According to the dictionary, to *discover* is to obtain insight or knowledge the first time, to ascertain, unearth, explore. A discoverer is one who finds out things for himself.

William Barclay, in his book *Daily Celebration,* says, "It is only when truth is discovered that it is appropriated. When a man is simply told the truth, it remains external to him and he can quite easily forget it. When he is led to discover the truth himself it becomes an integral part of him and he never forgets." The pattern in many Bible study groups is for the leader to be the *discoverer* and share his discoveries with others. Since the participants are not helped to become discoverers, they can quickly forget what was taught. My hope is that through the suggestions in this resource, you will learn how to become your own discoverer and never forget what you discover in God's Word.

Maybe you think that this emphasis on Bible study skills sounds cold and unspiritual. Can't a person just read the Bible and let the Holy Spirit guide us in discovering truths? Won't emphasis on skills make Bible study too mechanical and unspiritual?

It is very possible to learn the skills in study and come out only with intellectual knowledge, but this need not be, nor is it likely to happen. The pianist or the star baseball player is the one who has mastered the skills of playing so that mechanics have become second nature and he is free to play his best. In the same way, when you learn some of these rather mechanical skills of study, you will gain deeper insights into the truths in the Bible and the Holy Spirit will have a freer course in your life.

Practice, patience, and perseverance are needed for learning any skill. As you practice the skills described in this book, I am confident that gradually you will experience

- the joy of discovering truths in the Bible yourself.
- the joy of realizing that the Bible has something special to say to you personally.
- the joy of discovering your own potentials as a student.
- the joy of sharing with others the truths which have special meaning to you.
- the joy of knowing that the Holy Spirit is the Revealer of truth as you seek to discover it in his Word.
- the joy of discovering Jesus Christ as the incarnate Word.

Discovering with Others

You can become a *discoverer* in Bible study by yourself. It is possible to follow the suggestions in this resource and learn some of the keys to Bible study. But you can multiply the effectiveness of your study by working together with others in a small group. If you are using this book with a group in a congregation or school situation, you are already involved with others in the study. If you are all alone and want to use this resource, invite three or four others to study with you.

The traditional pattern for many Bible studies has been for the "students" to learn from the "teacher." The leader was the expert. Possibly the leader would involve the student in discussion, but in the main he or she was the chief resource. This is what we might call "leader–student learning." Students learned from the leader.

In discovery Bible study we want to involve you in "student–team learning." While you may still have a *leader* to be your guide, your most significant learning will be from persons in your small group—from your team members. Even though you are in a large class, you should work together in small teams of about four. This is how you work together as teams:

1. Each of you works individually on the suggested practice exercises in each section entitled Discovery Skills.
2. Then you come together and share with one another your insights, enlarging your understanding as you share.
3. Sometimes you may divide the tasks and each concentrate on only one segment of a passage. This way you can do a more thorough study and gain greater insights as you share and receive from the others.
4. The role of the leader is to be your *enabler*—the one who enables the members of your group to become discoverers and sharers.

Value of Team Learning

DEVELOPS SELF-RESPONSIBILITY: Team learning helps you exercise self-responsibility for your own learning. But it also calls for shared responsibility on the part of your teammates. You cannot expect to learn from one another until you first do some discovering yourself.

REQUIRES SELF-COMMITMENT: Team learning requires self-commitment on the part of all the team members. If you do no individual study, you will have nothing to share with your team members, and you will receive little from what they tell you. In the measure that you invest time in individual study, you will be enabled both to share and receive.

INCREASES SATISFACTION AND LEARNING: Two heads are better than one. As all of you study a segment, you will find that each one of you will discover different things. Your satisfaction will be derived first through your own discoveries and secondly through those received from others. No person can ever discover all of the riches in God's Word by himself.

DEVELOPS YOUR CREATIVE POTENTIAL. Team learning can help you develop your creative potential. Like many persons, you may have a low opinion of yourself as a student. By practicing some of the skills described in this resource, you will find you can discover some of the truths in Scripture and that others are enriched with your discoveries. Effective team learning is dependent on the willingness of all members to study, to share, to listen, to challenge and question each other. Through this process you will learn to clarify your own thinking, refine your insights, broaden your concepts, and correct faulty ones. You will discover that you have much more potential as a student than you realized.

NOTE: Read Chapter 14—*Discovering with Others,* for a more detailed discussion on the value of discovering Bible truths together with others.

CHAPTER 2

How to Become a Discoverer

Attitudes Toward Bible Study

If you wish to become a discoverer, one of your first needs is to consider the attitudes which will hinder or help you. As one Bible scholar has stated, too many people suffer from an inferiority complex when they approach Bible study. Let us list some of the attitudes which can help or hinder you in becoming a discoverer.

Faulty Attitudes

THE DEFEATED: I won't be able to understand anything anyway, so why try to study the Bible?

THE NEGATIVE: I would like to learn how to study the Bible better, but I doubt if anything I discover would be any good or right. I am afraid to express my ideas because I fear they will be wrong.

THE CLOSED HEART: I don't believe everything the Bible teaches. Since it was written so many hundreds of years ago, how can it have any value today? So why study it?

THE LAZY: I suppose if I tried I could understand more than I do, but what I read seems rather hard and dull. I don't know if I want to invest the energy to learn how to study.

Helpful Attitudes

THE POSITIVE: I want to learn how to study the Bible. No doubt I will have trouble learning some of the Bible study skills. I am sure there will be things in the Bible I'll not understand. But I believe that through the help of the Holy Spirit I too can learn how to gain insight into God's Word.

THE RECEPTIVE: God asks of me only an open heart and an open mind so that he can reveal himself and his truths to me. I don't have to understand everything.

THE EXPECTANT: I am coming to God's Word to let him speak to me. It is good to know that I don't have to inject ideas into my reading or to try to squeeze truths out of it. As I study and pray, I believe that the message in any Scripture passage will unfold itself to me.

THE FAITHFUL: I cannot expect much from Bible study unless I am willing to invest some energy and discipline in the study. I realize that God has placed a price on his Word: faithfulness and diligence in study. If I only scratch the surface, my reward is a few crumbs. If I dig deeply into the Word, my reward will be rich treasures.

Approaches to Bible Study

Usually you study the Bible with some definite purpose in mind. Possibly you have been invited to conduct a Bible study at a meeting or you are to teach a church school class. Or you may be studying it on your own for your personal inspiration. Whatever your reason, there are several approaches you can use.

HIT-AND-MISS APPROACH: You might approach your study in a hit-and-miss fashion. Maybe you read a passage several times. You may write down some of the ideas you gain in the reading. You may read it in another translation or look in a commentary. You may spend some time thinking and praying about what you read. You have no logical pattern that you follow.

THE APPLICATION APPROACH: This is one of the most common approaches. You quickly read the passage and then spend your time thinking about ways it might be applied to life.

THE COMMENTARY APPROACH: You read the Bible passage and then immediately read some commentaries for further insight. You let the commentary be your teacher.

THE HOLY SPIRIT APPROACH: This varies from the others in that you spend most of your study time in prayer and meditation. You read the passage and then look to the Holy Spirit to reveal to you the insights and truths in the passage without doing any serious study.

THE METHODICAL APPROACH: In this type you follow an orderly and logical pattern as you study your Bible. This approach does not discount the validity of the other approaches but incorporates them where appropriate. The methodical approach is not limited just to Bible study. The farmer follows a methodical pattern as he plants his crops. The cook follows definite steps as she prepares her dough for bread or batter for cake. Both know that the mechanics in the process will do much to insure the success of the product. Method is as important in Bible study as it is in farming or baking. As a Bible student, if you hope to become a discoverer, you need to develop an orderly and logical procedure in your study. In doing so you will find that you gain more insight and receive much greater satisfaction in your study than if you proceed in a hit-and-miss fashion or let the commentary be your teacher.

Process in Methodical Bible Study

Method implies a regular order. If you desire to develop a methodical pattern in your study of the Bible, there are definite procedures to follow, and it is best if they are done in a certain order. On the next page we have listed some of the procedures in Bible study and their most logical order. These processes are true in all study, not just Bible study. They lead from one to another and overlap each other. As you read the list, think about how you follow these procedures even when you are reading the daily newspaper.

Why This Emphasis on Logical Steps?

Maybe you are saying that you see no real sense in following such a logical procedure, that it makes Bible study so mechanical. We admit that there is a danger of method becoming an end in itself and that we cannot separate the study process into neat categories. Often one process overlaps with another. You will find that while one process leads into another, the procedure will be like a spiral in which you come back to previous processes. Interpretation will help you gain new insights into observations; summarization and application will give you additional insights into both observation and interpretation.

But there is real value in deliberately trying to do one process at the time. Most of us have a one-track mind. We accomplish the most when we concentrate on one thing at the time. This is especially true when we first try to understand something, whether it is a piece of literature or a scientific problem.

The scientist makes no interpretation and draws no conclusions until he has observed thoroughly all the facts. So it should be with you as a Bible student. First *observe!* No interpreting, no applying—until you have observed carefully what the author has written, observed *all* he has written!

This emphasis on the logical approach does not discount the importance of the Holy Spirit as the Revealer of truth. We need his guidance as we observe, interpret, evaluate, apply, and actualize. He is a part of the entire process, enabling us to be alert in our observations, discerning in our interpretations, honest in our evaluations and application and courageous in actualizing the truths in our own lives.

13

Procedures in Bible Study

1. OBSERVE exactly what the author is saying.	This is the most important step in Bible study and must come first. The more careful and thorough your observations, the more meaningful will be your interpretations, the fairer will be your evaluations, and the richer will be your applications.
2. INTERPRET objectively what the author has written.	After you have observed carefully what the author is saying, determine what he really meant by what he said. You are to try to discover the thoughts, attitudes, emotions, purpose of the author.
3. SUMMARIZE concisely the key ideas in a passage.	While summarization is listed as Step 3, it really is a process which should be done in connection with both observation and interpretation. Try to summarize the facts you observe and then the meaning of the facts.
4. EVALUATE fairly what the author has written.	Not until you have a clear concept of what the author has written and what he meant by what he wrote can you honestly judge the validity of the passage. Thus evaluation must come ofter observation and interpretation.
5. APPLY personally the message revealed.	While application is listed fifth in the process, this does not mean that it is fifth in importance. Application is the fruit which will come forth through the other processes. Application is a growing process, not superimposed in a superficial way, but rising out of all the other processes.
6. ACTUALIZE your convictions.	Someone has said, "Don't just study the Bible, *do* something!" Too often Bible study is mainly intellectualizing and emotionalizing the truths, but no actualizing— actually doing what the Lord revealed to us.

Tools for Bible Study

A BASIC STUDY BIBLE: You should use an accepted standard version for your basic study Bible. If your Bible is old and has small print, buy a new one. There are many basic versions to select from such as the *King James, Revised Standard Version, New English Bible, New American Standard, Jerusalem Bible, The New International Version.* All of these are based on original manuscripts. The translators have tried to be as accurate as possible in translating from the early manuscripts. All of the illustrations used in this resource will be taken from the *Revised Standard Version.*

SEVERAL TRANSLATIONS AND PARAPHRASES: Besides one basic study Bible, you should have several other translations. Among these you might want to have some of the more "free" translations and paraphrases, such as *The Living Bible, Today's English Version* (Good News for Modern Man), *Phillips,* or *Amplified Version.* All of these will give you insight into the meaning of words. It is possible to secure four to eight translations in a volume.

CONCORDANCE: A concordance is an alphabetical index to help you find Bible passages on particular subjects. While you do not need a large concordance, you may have one in the back of one of your Bibles. You need a concordance for finding cross-references.

DICTIONARY: A dictionary is a very important tool in Bible study. Looking up definitions of key words will give you new insight into meanings.

COMMENTARIES, BIBLE DICTIONARY, BIBLE ATLAS: These are very helpful in providing background to the geography, background, and culture of the Bible times, as well as insight into some of the difficult passages. These are listed last and should be used last in the process of interpretation.

CHAPTER 3

Begin by
Learning to See!

The first skill you need to develop is to train your mind to *see* when you read a passage—to observe carefully the words, to be on the alert for the details. Too many of us are in the habit of reading Scripture without seeing very much, without thinking about the words we are seeing. We read words, but we do not observe what the words are saying. Sometimes we do not even see all the words in a passage. We are lazy observers! Because of inaccurate and careless observations, we often make faulty interpretations and shallow applications.

Meaning and Purpose of Observation

Observation can be defined in several ways: the act, power, or habit of seeing and noting; thorough and careful notice; to watch closely; to look intently; to give full attention to what one sees; to be mentally aware of what one sees. One person described observation as "the art of seeing things as they are, impartially, intensely, fearlessly."

Observation demands concentration!

The purpose of observation is to saturate yourself thoroughly with the content of a passage. Like a sponge you should absorb everything that is before you. You need to learn to be exact and accurate in your observations. Not everything you read will be of equal value; therefore, in the process you also have to learn to discern what is noteworthy and what is not. All of these procedures require concentration.

Ways to Observe

One reason we do not "see" very much when we read is that we do not know what to look for. Most of us need "handles" or "clues," help in knowing what specific things to look for. Once we learn what are some of the specific things to observe, we will begin to discover things in our reading that we never saw before.

Learning to observe details is a skill which will take time and practice. On the next two pages are charts containing lists of the kinds of things to look for when reading a passage. This list is a quick overview. In the following chapters, they will be described in greater detail. This list will have little meaning to you until you become involved in looking for some of these clues to discovering what an author is saying.

Observations Overwhelming?

As you study the lists on the following pages, the specific things for which to look when trying to develop your powers of observation, you may feel overwhelmed. Possibly you are asking yourself, "How can I be alert for all of these things? There are too many things to look for at one time!"

We have listed many things in order to acquaint you with the variety of things for which to be alert, but learning to observe is like any other skill. You will learn it a step at a time.

One of the most difficult problems in helping persons to develop their powers of observation is to get them to believe that it has value. Some persons feel that it is a waste of time. They feel that application is the most important aspect of Bible study. They want to read a passage quickly and then spend their time concentrating on how to apply the message. Others just want to focus on interpretation, trying to find out what the commentaries have to say about a passage.

Learning the skills in observation can be a rather frustrating process. Careful observation requires concentrated thinking, and few of us really want to learn how to think! Someone has said that five percent of the people *think*. Fifteen percent of the people *think they think*. Eighty percent of the people would rather *die than think*. This may be an unfair judgment, but I challenge you to remember these words when you become frustrated in learning how to develop your powers of observation.

Practice Skills

To learn the skills of observation takes practice. While we listed many things, you will practice only a few at a time. Gradually as you practice, you will find observing details to become second nature. On pages 20-24 are some Discovery Skills for you to practice. Don't just read the suggestions. Actually do them, one practice skill at a time. You will soon find how quickly your power of observation increases as you follow the suggestions.

Specific Things to Observe

Key Words	When you first read a passage, look for the key words, those words which you think are important in the passage. Repetition of words will sometimes give you a clue. Underline them in your Bible.
Advice **admonitions** **warnings** **promises**	Be on the alert for the admonitions which a writer gives: the advice, the exhortations, the warnings, the things which he tells you to do. Also note the promises and the encouragements. One clue is to look for imperative verbs.
Reasons **Results** **for** **doing things**	When you observe admonitions, see if the writer gives you some reasons for his advice. Or note if he sets forth a *cause-and-effect* relationship — *if you do this*, *then* this will happen. Often with a warning, he will give possible results.
contrasts **comparisons** **illustrations**	Make special note of the way a writer uses contrasts, comparisons, illustrations to bring out his ideas. Comparison is the association of things that are similar. Contrast is the association of things that are opposite, often introduced with "but."
Repetition **and** **progression** **of ideas**	Be on the alert for repetition of words, ideas, statements. This will often give you a clue as to the author's purpose in a passage. Take special note of lists of items or ideas. Compare the items and see if there is any significance in the order. Do ideas progress toward a climax?
Questions	Be on the watch for the use of the question. Is it used to introduce an idea, summarize a series of ideas, or just to challenge the thinking?

Specific Things to Observe

Important connectives prepositions conjunctions	Connectives are very important in revealing key ideas and relationships. Be on the alert for some of the following: *but*—introduces a contrast *if*—introduces conditional clause *for, because, therefore*—introduce reason and results *in, into, with*—important connectives *in order that*—sets forth a purpose
Grammatical construction verbs nouns pronouns adverbs adjectives	The term "grammar" no doubt frightens you, but even so, it is important to note the grammatical construction of some statements. Be on the alert for the verbs and their tenses—for the use of pronouns—for the use of adverbs and adjectives and the way they describe things.
Atmosphere **Emphatic statements**	Note the general tone of a passage. It may be characterized by the mood of joy, thanksgiving, concern, humility, zeal, anger, caution. The tone of a passage may vary as a writer moves from one idea to another. The mood of a writer is often revealed by the way he addresses his readers. Also note the use he makes of emphatic statements, words and phrases to reveal his feelings.
Literary form	Always note the literary form of a passage — discourse, narrative, poetic, dramatic, parabolic, apocalyptic. Also determine if the writer is using literal or figurative terms.
General structure	Note the arrangement of the ideas in a passage, the relationship of verses to each other. Sometimes the author makes a general statement, then explains it with examples. Other times he may list a series of ideas and then summarize with a general statement.

Practice A — Be on Alert for Details

1. Look for key words

No matter what you are reading, the first step is always to be on the alert for the key words, those words which seem to you to be important words to the message. This is one of the easier processes in observation, but also is one of the most important. Whether you are reading the Bible, a book, a magazine, or a newspaper, you have to begin by observing the *words* and decide which seem to be the most important for understanding the main thrust of the passage.

On page 21 is a "structural diagram" of Matthew 6:25-34. This is the passage you are to use for your first practice. Note the way the units of thought are arranged so that it is easier to see what is in the passage. As you study this passage, make your observations directly on the printed passage.

a) UNDERLINE THE KEY WORDS. As you begin to read Matthew 6:25-34, using a colored pencil, underline what you consider some of the key words. One of the clues is to note the words which are repeated. Do not be afraid to underline anything you feel is important. There is no right or wrong when underlining what you consider important words. Underline as many as you feel like underlining. Be sure you do this step before you begin the next step.

b) SELECT THE MOST IMPORTANT WORDS. In the process you may have underlined many words, or just a few, because you were not sure just how to select key words. If you have underlined many, your next task is to determine which of the many are *the* key words. Not all of the words which you may have underlined have equal value. Review those which you have underlined and select about four which you feel are most significant in terms of the message in the passage. Circle these words.

2. Look for other details

Looking for key words has given you some insight into the passage, but this is just a beginning. To gain more insight, here are some other things to do. If you are several in your small study group, divide the verses among you: 6:25-27; 28-30; 31-34. Record in the left margin of the passage other things you observe.

    a) admonitions and reasons
    b) use of questions
    c) contrasts, comparisons, illustrations
    d) key connectives *(circle these)*
    f) repetition of ideas
    g) emphatic statements

25. "Therefore I tell you,
　　do not be anxious about your life,
　　　what you shall eat or
　　　what you shall drink,
　　nor about your body,
　　　what you shall put on.

　Is not life more than food,
　　and the body more than clothing?

26. Look at the birds of the air:
　　they neither sow nor reap
　　　nor gather into barns,
　　and yet your heavenly Father feeds them.

　Are you not of more value than they?

27. And which of you by being anxious
　　can add one cubit to his span of life?

28. And why are you anxious about clothing?
　　Consider the lilies of the field,
　　　how they grow;
　　　　they neither toil nor spin;

29. yet I tell you,
　　even Solomon in all his glory
　　　was not arrayed like one of these.

30. But if God so clothes the grass of the field,
　　which today is alive
　　　and tomorrow is thrown into the oven,
　　will he not much more clothe you,
　　　O men of little faith?

31. Therefore, do not be anxious, saying,
　　'What shall we eat?'
　　　or 'What shall we drink?'
　　　or 'What shall we wear?'

32. For the Gentiles seek all these things;
　　and your heavenly Father knows
　　　that you need them all.

33. But seek first his kingdom and his righteousness,
　　and all these things
　　　shall be yours as well.

34. Therefore, do not be anxious about tomorrow,
　　for tomorrow will be anxious for itself.
　Let the day's own trouble
　　be sufficient for the day."

Example

Observations	Scripture Passage
Important connective — *therefore*	25. "Therefore I tell you,
emphatic statement—*I tell you*	do not be anxious about
Admonition — *do not be anxious*	your life,
key words—*anxious*—*life*	what you shall eat or
two illustrations—*eat*—*drink*	what you shall drink,
body—second thing not to be	nor about your body,
anxious about	what you shall put on.
Note use of question.	Is not life more than food,
Note repetition of words: *life,*	and body more than
body, more	clothing?"

This is an example of how you might record observations on the printed Bible passage. You might not have room to put down all that I have included. You might record the observation and draw a line to the word or group of words about which you are making the observation.

3. Look for general structure

Remember that one of the things to observe is the general structure of a passage—the relationship of the verses to each other. Again study this passage and bracket those verses which seem to focus on the same topic. If you have not done much analyzation of structure, I will give you one way to bracket the verses: 6:25; 26-27; 28-30; 31-34. Then summarize the main idea in each set of verses in brief phrases.

This passage is an example of progression on ideas. Determine which verse is the climax of the passage.

Practice B — Seek to Know Meanings

1. Begin by asking yourself questions

You have been involved in several experiences to help you develop your powers of observation. You have just begun to develop them. This is a process which takes time and practice. But even in the little practice you have had, you may have become aware of another process which has been developing. Possibly you have been asking yourself some questions, such as: "I wonder why Jesus said the things he did? I wonder what he meant by what he said?" Asking yourself questions is a very important step in Bible study—in any kind of study. It is the bridge between observation and interpretation. These questions might be called, "I wonder questions" or "questions for understanding."

Maybe you are saying, "But what kind of questions do I ask? I have never thought much about asking myself questions." Learning to ask ourselves questions about what we read is a skill just like learning how to observe. At first most persons do not know how to ask themselves questions. In Chapter 6 we shall focus more intently on the process of asking questions, but in this practice we shall list some of the kinds you can ask yourself:

- Why did Jesus say . . . ?
- What is the meaning of . . . ?
- What is the significance of . . . ?
- What is the implication of . . . ?
- What is the relationship between . . . ?

Since you may not have had much practice in asking questions, I shall list some of the kinds you might ask yourself in terms of the passage. Begin by asking questions about key words, even though you think you know their meaning.

Example

Scripture Passage	Questions for Understanding
25. "Therefore I tell you, do not be anxious about your life,	Why the emphatic words, *I tell you?* Meaning of *anxious?* Meaning of *life?*
what you shall eat or what you shall drink,	Significance of these illustrations?
nor about your body, what you shall put on.	Meaning of *body?* Significance of this illustration?
Is not life more than food and the body more than clothing?"	Significance of this question? Symbolic meaning of *food* and *clothing?*

These are samples of the kinds of questions you might ask yourself. If you focused on only a few of the verses in the process of observation, focus on the same verses and record some of the questions you might ask yourself about the observations you made.

2. Answering questions

The asking of questions has several purposes: to stimulate your thinking and to begin to identify those words, phrases, and statements which need interpretation. Maybe you thought such words as, *anxious, body, life,* were words you already knew and did not need interpretation. But when you begin to ask yourself questions about them, you realize that you need to interpret them in order to understand the passage.

In Chapter 6 we shall discuss more thoroughly the ways to interpret a passage, but in this chapter we suggest only a few of the ways. If you are working with a small group, again divide your task. Each person could work on one section of the verses for interpretation. Try to answer some of the questions by doing these things:

a) DEFINE WORDS: Look in a dictionary to discover what is the meaning of some of the key words such as: *anxious, life, body, kingdom, righteousness.*

b) COMPARE TRANSLATIONS: Read the passage in several translations to discover what other words are used in translating the passage.

c) STUDY CROSS-REFERENCES: Look up some of these cross-references for additional insight into meanings: Luke 12:22-31; Romans 14:17; Phil. 4:4-7.

d) WRESTLE WITH MEANINGS: This last suggestion is a very important part in Bible study. It is possible to define words, compare translations, study cross-references, and still not really get at the core of the meaning of a passage. You also have to wrestle, think, meditate, integrate what you have been learning, and draw conclusions.

e) SUMMARIZE FINDINGS: Try to formulate the insights gained through your study in some summary statements: Jesus seems to be saying in this verse or group of verses these things . . .

Practice C — Personalize Biblical Teachings

This is a passage which speaks to the basic needs of life. All of us are plagued with anxieties about "food" and "clothing"—the very necessities of life. Jesus seems to be focusing on priorities, that which we are to place first in our lives. If we give him the proper place in our lives, we can trust him to take care of all our *needs*—although he may not supply all our *wants*.

Evaluation

As you have studied this passage, you need to ask yourself if what Jesus says has value for today. If we place Jesus first in our lives, will he really supply all our needs?

Application and Actualization

Select one of the following and consider how you might apply the challenge in this passage to your life:

1. Complete this statement: If I really took Jesus' teaching in this passage seriously, the difference it would make in my life is . . .

2. Analyze your anxieties. Divide a sheet of paper in three parts:

List some things you are anxious about right now.	List some of the ways you usually handle your anxieties.	Following Jesus' admonitions, list some ways that would be better approaches.

3. Study the advertisements in papers. What do they say to us about priorities and anxieties?

4. Share and pray. Share with your teammates an anxiety which you now have and invite them to pray with you about it. Pray with them about theirs.

CHAPTER 4

How to Increase Your Powers of Observation

You have just practiced the main procedures which are involved in any Bible study, steps which you need follow to discover the content and meaning of a passage. As you studied Matthew 6:25-34, you did these things:

Observed—by looking for key words, admonitions, questions, contrasts, comparisons, illustrations, connectives, etc.

Interpreted—by asking questions, comparing translations, defining words, studying cross-references, wrestling with meanings.

Summarized—by bracketing verses and summarizing key ideas.

Evaluated—by determining what value Jesus' words have for persons today.

Applied—by thinking of what these words were saying to you personally.

Actualized—only you know in what way you have been actualizing the admonitions in this passage.

Problems?

When you tried to follow some of these steps, did you have problems? If you did, you are normal! Learning skills takes practice. But I hope you did gain a deeper insight into this passage, even though it is a passage you may have read many times. Through some of these experiences, I hope that you were helped to become a discoverer, that you discovered some truths which you had not discovered before in your reading.

You have just begun to use some of the techniques which will increase your powers of observation. In Chapter 3 you were given a list of the many things for which you can look. A very brief description was given of each one. In order to broaden your understanding of these techniques we shall review the list and give a more detailed description of some of them. After you have studied the more detailed descriptions, you are to work on another passage for practicing.

1. Look for admonitions.

When you are reading a discourse passage, be on the alert for every time the writer tells you to *do something* or *not to do something* or *to be something*. These might be admonitions, warnings, exhortations, advice, commands, promises. The writer will be speaking directly to you, the reader. Or in the case of Jesus' admonitions, he will be speaking directly to his hearers. When you look for admonitions, note the imperative verbs, those which tell you to do something. These are often your key.

2. Look for logical relationships.

Whenever a writer gives *commands* or *advice* or *warnings,* he will often back them up with *reasons, purposes, proofs* or *results.* Also be on the alert for *cause-and-effect* relationships. Sometimes the writer will set forth a warning and then show the effects if the warning is not heeded. Or he may describe a condition and then give the reason for the condition. Connectives are often the key for noting logical relationships. Train yourself to observe these key connectives:

because or *for:* These words often introduce a reason or result.

in order that: This phrase often sets forth a purpose.

therefore: This word often introduces a summary of ideas, a result or condition.

if: This conjunction introduces a condition which requires action or sets forth a cause which will bring forth certain results. *"If* this is true, *then* this will happen or this should happen."

3. Look for contrasts, comparisons, illustrations.

When a writer seeks to convey a new idea, he will often try to associate it with something that is already familiar to the reader. Make special note of the way a writer uses contrasts, comparisons, and illustrations to bring out his ideas. A comparison is the association of similar things. In grammar we speak of "similes" and "metaphors." An example of a simile is: "The tongue is *like* a fire." An example of a metaphor is: "The tongue *is* a fire."

A contrast is the association of opposites. We are told that our minds can recall contrasts better than we recall comparisons. The connective "but" often introduces a contrast.

4. Look for repetitions and progressions in thought.

In order to impress his readers and communicate his ideas, an author will often repeat words, phrases, ideas. These you will often discover as you look for key words.

Also make special note of lists of items. Authors have reasons for listing what they do and even for the order of a series. You should study the series to see if there is any significance in the order of the list or progression in thought. Compare the first and the last items in a series to see if there is any significant difference.

There can be progression in thought patterns as well as in a series of items. One idea can grow out of another. Note how the author arranges his material so that the ideas progress toward a climax. Does he build one idea on another until he presents his greatest challenge at the end of a paragraph or chapter?

5. Look for grammatical constructions.

The term grammar may frighten you, but it is important to make note of some grammatical constructions. Let us not forget that some of our Christian doctrines have been determined by the grammatical use of verb tenses, singular nouns, and little prepositions such as "in" and "through."

You do not have to identify every word in a passage in terms of its grammatical construction, but the following list reflects some of the areas for which to be alert:

- *Nouns* and *pronouns:* Especially be mindful of the personal pronouns.
- *Verbs and their tenses:* Verbs are often key to understanding a passage.
- *Adjectives and adverbs:* Note what they describe.
- *Key prepositions:* Note the significance of such words as *in, through, into, by, of.*
- *Important connectives:* Be mindful of the connectives which reflect results, reasons and conclusions, such as, *therefore, yet, however, likewise, nevertheless.*
- *Emphatic words:* Note words and phrases which the author uses to give emphasis to his thoughts such as, *truly, verily, behold, indeed, finally, especially, last of all, I tell you.*
- *Phrases* and *clauses:* Note what they describe. Note how some clauses are introduced with the words, *who, where, when, what, why, how.* These are also words which you might use as questions when you are observing a passage.

Don't be discouraged by this list. You will find that as you look for other things, you will begin to identify some of these grammatical constructions as well.

6. Look for use of questions.

Always be on the watch for the use of questions. An author may use a question to introduce an idea, or to challenge the thinking of the readers, or to summarize his ideas at the close. Sometimes he may use what is called a "rhetorical question." He does not expect an answer, but uses it just to stimulate the thinking of the reader and challenge him in his response.

7. Look for the general structure of passage.

Be mindful of the structure of a biblical passage, whether it is a paragraph, a chapter, or even a book. Structure can often reveal an author's purpose. When a person writes something, he usually has a definite purpose for what he says. Therefore, he will not only be concerned about the words he uses, but also about the way he arranges his ideas. Sometimes he may arrange his ideas in a logical order, one idea growing out of the next. He reveals his concern for his intellectual impact. Other times he will arrange his ideas in a psychological order, revealing his concern for the emotional impact. Sometimes, Bible passages seem to have no apparent order in terms of structure. The ideas are more like beads on a string, or they tumble out in profusion like Paul's ideas in some of his epistles.

Always be on the alert for the relationship of verses and paragraphs to each other. Make note of those verses which seem to focus on the same ideas. Also note whether an author begins with a general statement and then explains it with specific examples, or if he begins with a series of ideas and then summarizes with a general statement.

8. Look for literary form and atmosphere.

Literary form is the type of writing an author uses to express his message. The major types which authors can use are found in biblical literature. As you study a passage, observe the following types:

Discourse—the kind of approach found in Jesus' sermons and employed in the epistles, in which ideas are presented in logical and argumentative form.

Prose narrative—found in the historical books and the Gospels, where historical events are often described in chronological order.

Poetry—the type found in the Psalms and Job.

Parable—brief stories used to bring out a specific truth, like the parables of Jesus.

Apocalyptic—characterized by symbolism and descriptions of visions, as in the book of Revelation and Daniel.

Also you need to discern whether the author is using *literal* or *figurative* terminology. A literal term is one that is to be considered according to its natural or usual meaning. A figurative term is symbolic in nature and must be interpreted accordingly. For instance, when Jesus said, "I am the living bread . . . if any man eat of this bread, he shall live forever" (John 6:51), he was using figurative language. The Jews who heard him interpreted his words literally and asked, "How can the man give us his flesh to eat?" (John 6:52). So it is when you observe and interpret. Unless you observe and understand the nature of the terminology, you may be unfair to the author in your interpretations.

The general tone of a passage is also important to observe. It may be characterized by the mood of joy, thanksgiving, concern, humility, zeal, anger, despair. You can sense the feelings of an author, by the words he uses and the way he puts his words together.

Practice A — Observe the Details

1. Look for key words

On page 30 is a "structural diagram" of 1 Corinthians 13. This is the passage which you are to use for your practice this time. Make your observations directly on the printed page.

First, read the passage and underline what you consider to be some of the key words. It is not difficult to select *the* key word in this passage, but also select three or four others which you think are also keys to the message of the chapter. Remember that your selections might differ from those which others select.

2. Look for other details

Reread the passage and note the many literary techniques Paul used to convey his message. Note that Paul gives no admonitions in this passage, but he makes strong use of some other approaches. If there are several in your group, each of you might study just one section of verses.

a) CAUSE-AND-EFFECT RELATIONSHIPS: See how many examples of these you can find. Remember the little word *if* is one of your clues.

b) CONTRASTS: This is a passage in which there are many contrasts. See how many contrasts you can identify. Make your notes in the left margin of the passage. Circle key connectives.

c) COMPARISONS AND ILLUSTRATIONS: Note what use he makes of these.

d) REPETITIONS AND PROGRESSION OF THOUGHT: This passage has several examples of repetition of thought patterns and listing of items. Make note of the repetitions. Study the listing of items. Does there seem to be a progression of thought? Is there a climax?

e) DESCRIPTION: Note the positive and negative aspects of love.

f) GRAMMATICAL CONSTRUCTIONS: Study the verbs in the passage. What do you note about their tenses? Also note the personal pronouns. When are they used, and when are they not used?

3. Analyze the structure

Study the verses and bracket those which seem to focus on the same idea. The diagram itself provides a clue for bracketing. Try to summarize the main idea in each section with a phrase.

Consider also the order in which Paul arranged his ideas. Are they arranged logically or psychologically?

1. If I speak in the tongues of men and of angels,
    but have not love,
        I am a noisy gong or a clanging cymbal.

2. And if I have prophetic powers,
    and understand all mysteries and all knowledge,
    and if I have all faith, so as to remove mountains,
    but have not love,
        I am nothing.

3. If I give away all I have,
    and if I deliver my body to be burned,
    but have not love,
        I gain nothing.

4. Love is patient and kind;
    love is not jealous or boastful;

5. it is not arrogant or rude.
    Love does not insist on its own way;
    it is not irritable or resentful;

6. it does not rejoice at wrong,
    but rejoices in the right.

7. Love bears all things,
    believes all things,
        hopes all things,
            endures all things.

8. Love never ends;
    as for prophecies, they will pass away;
    as for tongues, they will cease;
    as for knowledge, it will pass away.

9. For our knowledge is imperfect
    and our prophecy is imperfect;

10. but when the perfect comes,
    the imperfect will pass away.

11. When I was a child,
    I spoke like a child,
        I thought like a child,
            I reasoned like a child;
    when I became a man,
        I gave up childish ways.

12. For now we see in a mirror dimly,
    but then face to face.
    Now I know in part;
        then I shall understand fully,
            even as I have been fully understood.

13. So faith, hope, love abide, these three;
    but the greatest of these is love.

Practice B — Seek to Know Meanings

1. Ask yourself questions

While you may be very familiar with this passage and even have memorized it, you still need to think seriously about what Paul means by the words he is saying. So far, you have only been observing the details, but hopefully you have also been asking yourself some "I wonder" questions about the meaning of some of the words and statements. Our concern is what Paul meant by what he said. Let us review some of the kinds of questions you might be asking yourself:

- Why did Paul say . . . ?
- What is the meaning of . . . ?
- What is the significance of . . . ?
- What is the implication of . . . ?
- What is the relationship between . . . ?

Example

Scripture Passage	Questions for Understanding
1. If I speak in the tongues of men and of angels,	Why the emphasis on *angels* as well as *men*? Why begin with the conditional clause, "If I . . ."?
but have not love,	Meaning of *love*? Meaning of *noisy gong? clanging cymbal?* Significance of these illustrations? Significance of present tense verb, *I am*
I am a noisy gong or a clanging cymbal.	Relationship between *have not love* and being a *noisy gong?*

I have given you an example of the kinds of questions you might ask yourself about statements and words in the first verse.

If there are several in your group, divide the sections of the chapter among you so that you work with only a few of the verses. Ask yourself some "questions for understanding," and record these in the right margin of the printed copy of the chapter. Then share these questions with those in your group.

2. Answering questions

Remember that the asking of questions is to stimulate your thinking and to serve as a guide for identifying those words, phrases, and statements which need interpretation. You may ask more questions than you can or need to answer. You are to select those which seem to be the most relevant for answering. Surely in this passage, the key word *love* must be interpreted. What did Paul mean by the word *love?* But there are other statements which also need interpreting.

Select some of the questions you asked regarding one section of the chapter and seek to answer them by doing some of these things:
- *define* words;
- *compare* translations;
- *study* cross-references;
- *wrestle* with meanings.

In seeking to interpret the message of chapter, it is very important that you wrestle with meanings: What is Paul really trying to say as to the importance of love? Why did he arrange his thoughts in the order he did? Why does he describe both the positive and negative aspects of love?

NOTE: Read Chapter 6, "Ways to Interpret," to gain more detailed information on how to ask questions and how to interpret passages.

Practice C — Personalize Biblical Teachings

When Paul describes love, he approaches it in an impersonal way, "Love is . . ." But everything he says about love has to do with personal relationships—especially difficult personal relationships. Possibly this is the reason for the emphasis on the negative aspect—"Love is not . . ." We know that Paul is speaking about a special kind of love—*agape*—a self-giving love which God extends to us through Christ. But what about ourselves, how do we actualize it in our own lives?

Evaluation

Are Paul's statements in this chapter valid for our relationships of today?

Application and Actualization

Review 1 Corinthians 13:4-7. Consider seriously the way Paul describes what love is and what it is not.

1. Think about a problem situation in which there are conflicts, disagreements, misunderstandings—a real situation in which you have been involved or are now involved.

Present situation: What can you actually do if you are going to demonstrate these evidences of love as described in 13:4-7? What might be the outcomes?

Previous situation: To what extent did or did you not demonstrate these evidences of love? What were the results? How might the results have been different?

2. Share with your group a situation in which you need to demonstrate love. Invite them to pray with you about this situation.

NOTE: Read Chapter 13, "Personalizing Biblical Teachings," for more detailed discussion on how to apply and actualize biblical truths.

CHAPTER 5

Studying a Narrative

So far in your study, you have focused on what is called discourse literature—literature that focuses on ideas. You have studied one section of Jesus' Sermon on the Mount and one chapter in an epistle. Both of these passages were didactic in nature—that is both Jesus and Paul were trying to teach some important concepts. They used a variety of literary techniques to communicate their ideas.

To gain insight into the message of these passages, you were guided to look for some of these techniques. You were to look for key words, admonitions, cause-and-effect relationships, contrasts, comparisons, illustrations, and connectives. The methods you used with these two passages can be applied to all kinds of literature.

The Six Guide-Words

But there is still another way of observing a passage, especially a narrative, that will help you gain insight into the details of a story. You can use six words as your guides: *who, where, when, what, why, how.*

Let us consider how we might use these words as guides for observing the details of a narrative. Remember that they can also be used for observing any other kind of literature.

WHERE: Note the setting of a story. It is helpful to locate it on a map.

WHEN: Note the time element in a story. Sometimes you may have to study other passages to determine the time.

WHO: Note the characters in a story and how each is described.

WHAT: Note the exact order and details of the events, actions, and conversation of the characters. Sometimes you will find it helpful to list the events, the actions, and conversation in chronological order. Note the way characters respond to each other.

33

Read the story imaginatively, trying to build mental images, re-creating the story in your own mind. As you read, try to *see, hear, feel* what the characters *saw, heard,* and *felt*.

How: Note how the story ends, how the events and actions of the characters shaped the ending. Note how the characters act and respond as normal human beings. Note how they respond to each other.

Why: Observe more than mere words. Ask yourself some questions: Why did events happen as they did? Why did the characters act and respond as they did? Could they have responded differently?

Approach to a Narrative

Too often we approach a Bible narrative superficially. We may have heard the story so many times that it is commonplace to us. Or we think of the story only in terms of its message and forget that these Bible characters were real flesh-and-blood people who lived in a certain period of history. Because of the superficial way we approach the stories, we are also superficial in the way we interpret and apply them. Besides using the six guide-words, consider these additional approaches in your study.

Be realistic. As you study a Bible story, try to view it in the context of the historical setting of that day. Beware of viewing it through twentieth century glasses. Remember that in the biblical days there were no welfare programs, refrigeration, women's liberation, etc. For this reason it is important that you study about the laws, the religious teachings, the customs and practices of the day.

Be imaginative. Most Bible stories tell only the bare facts. As you read a story, give it "flesh and blood" in your imagination. Picture yourself as part of the scene. Visualize what you would be seeing and hearing. Try to see and hear not only the words and actions of Bible persons, but the tone of their voices, facial expressions, bodily responses.

Be empathic. *Empathy* means to identify with a person and his problems and his feelings. Try to place yourself in the "skin" of Bible characters, identifying with them and their emotions, yearnings, hurts, concerns, difficulties, joys. While it is not difficult to identify with outward actions and responses of Bible persons, try also to determine the inner emotions and needs which are reflected in the outer actions.

Practice A — Observe the Details

1. Study Luke 23:32-49

In order to practice the skills in the use of these six words as guides for observing details, you are to concentrate on a very familiar passage in Scripture, one of the accounts of Jesus' crucifixion.

First, read the section quickly and note these things:

WHERE: Note the places mentioned in the passage.

WHEN: Note the references to time.

WHO: Note the many persons mentioned in the account.

WHAT: Look for some key words in the statements that Jesus and other persons make.

2. Analyze carefully Luke 23:34-49

Your first reading should give you an overview of the main emphasis in the passage. Now make a more careful study of a part of the passage, noting especially how each person responds to Jesus. Divide a sheet of paper into four sections and record the details in chronological order.

Section 1: Record the WHOs—List the persons (other than Jesus) mentioned in the passage.

Section 2: Record WHAT they did relating to Jesus.

Section 3: Record HOW they responded to Jesus in terms of what they said. Note the titles they gave him and the pronouns they used relating to Jesus.

Section 4: Record HOW Jesus responded.

WHO (list persons)	WHAT they did	HOW they responded verbally	HOW Jesus responded

Practice B — Seek to Know Meanings

1. Build mental images

The account of Jesus' crucifixion is a dramatic story. As you study the account, try to imagine what it was like to be there. Recreate in your mind the scene and all the people involved. Try to *see, hear, feel* what the persons were *seeing, hearing, feeling.* Try to imagine the actions, the gestures, the way the persons said what they said.

Select one of the persons at the cross and share with your group how you think this person spoke and acted.

35

2. Ask yourself questions

a) ABOUT THE WORDS AND ACTIONS OF PERSONS:

- Any significance in the titles the different persons gave Jesus?

- Any significance in the pronouns they used? Note that the soldiers said "you" and the rulers said "he."

b) ABOUT KEY WORDS:

One of the key words in this passage is *save*. Note that the rulers, soldiers, and one criminal all use the word. Some questions you might ask yourself are:

- What does the word *save* mean?

- What did it mean to those who were speaking to Jesus?

3. Seek to find answers to questions

You might gain insight into the message of this narrative by doing some of these things:

a) *Define words:* Look up the word *save* in a dictionary. Think about its meaning and use.

b) *Cross-references:* Read the account of Jesus' crucifixion in other Gospels. Study the meaning of the titles given to Jesus.
Consider the use of the word *save* in these cross-references: Luke 19:10; John 12:47. What did Jesus mean by the word *save?*

c) *Translations:* Read the account in other translations to see if you gain additional insight.

Practice C — Personalize Biblical Teachings

The persons who witnessed the crucifixion reflect the many ways persons can respond to Jesus. They are a composite of humanity. They can represent the many kinds of people. But they can also represent the many ways each one of us can respond to Jesus at different times in our lives.

1. Identify responses

What kind of responses do the following reflect:

soldiers	rulers	second criminal
people	first criminal	centurion

2. Identify with a person

While it is easy to be judgmental of those at the cross, at different times in our lives, each one of us may have responded to Jesus in any one of these ways. Think about your present feelings and a problem or situation which you are facing. Identify with one person at the cross which reflects your response to Jesus *right now:*

_____ anger because Jesus is not doing what you want him to do

_____ watching on the sidelines, not getting too involved

_____ taking Jesus rather casually

_____ demanding that he "save" your situation

_____ feeling totally helpless, praying "remember me"

_____ praising him

_____ beating your breast

3. Meditate on this scene at the cross

Complete these statements:

One thing I can believe is . . .

One thing I have learned about relationships is . . .

The Good News I find in this scene at the cross is . . .

4. Pray about your response to Jesus

Invite the members in your group to pray with you about your response to Jesus.

Pray with them about their response to him.

DISCOVERY SKILLS IV   **Bible Focus: Matthew 13:1-9; 18-23**
(optional)

Purpose of Bible Study

As you have been learning these skills in how to study the Bible, you have been involved in three studies. Hopefully by now you have found that the learning of the skills has not been an end in itself, but a means by which you were enabled to gain deeper insights into the Word of God. But even deeper insights can become ends in themselves unless you have been responding to God's Word with open and receptive hearts.

Studying the Bible is never to be an end in itself, but the means by which you grow in faith and knowledge of God through Jesus Christ. The Bible might be described in two words: *revelation* and *response*. It is a record of God's revelation of himself to men through Jesus Christ and of man's response to this revelation. Its purpose is to enable men to come to know this revelation and respond in faith. John in his Gospel best describes the purpose of the Bible:

"Now Jesus did many other signs in the presence of the disciples, which are not written in this book; but these are written that you may believe that Jesus is the Christ, the Son of God, and that believing you may have life in his name" (John 20:30-31).

While the passages which you have studied may not seem related in any way, they all have to do with relationships and response.

Matthew 6:25-34: The focus is on our response to the kingdom of God in contrast to our response to the "things" of life.

1 Corinthians 13: The focus is on our response in personal relationships.

Luke 23:32-49: The focus is on our response to Jesus and his cross.

Since the emphasis in this book is on how to study the Bible, it seems appropriate to have one study on Jesus' parable of the sower and the four soils. The focus of this parable is on man's response to the Word of God itself.

Practice A — Observe the Details

1. Read Matthew 13:1-3.

As you study the introduction to the parable, continue with the techniques you used with your study of a narrative. As you read these first three verses, note the *who, where, when, what* of the introduction. Verbs are your clues as to *what* Jesus did.

2. Read Matthew 13:4-9.

As you read the parable, again use the six words for insight into the details:

WHO: The sower and the seed.

WHERE: Note the kinds of soil on which the seed fell.

WHAT: Note what happens to the seed in each illustration.

HOW: Note how the illustration ends in each case in terms of growth of the seed.

WHY: Note that in some illustrations Jesus gives a reason (vv. 5-6).

3. Read Matthew 13:18-23.

Note that you are to skip Matthew 13:10-17. This passage needs special study which we do not take the time for now. Concentrate just on Jesus' interpretation of the parable.

a) Read this section and underline what seem to be some of the key words. Select about four which you feel are the key words.

b) Make a special study of Jesus' interpretation of each of the illustrations. If there are several in your group, divide the illustrations among you, each taking one: 13:19; 13:20-21; 13:22; 13:23. With each of the illustrations you are to do the following:

WHO: The who in each illustration is *anyone* or *he*. Note how he responds to the Word.

WHAT: Note what happens to the word that is sown.

HOW: Note how the illustration ends.

WHY: Note if there are any reasons for the illustration ending as it does.

If you would like to record your observations, you might use the following pattern:

WHO (response to the Word)	WHAT happens to the Word	HOW the illustration ends	WHY (not always given)

Practice B — Seek to Know Meanings

1. Ask questions for understanding.

Hopefully, as you have been observing, you have also been asking yourself some questions. To guide you in the asking, here are some general ones to ask yourself:

a) *Definitions:* What is the meaning of some of the key words: *hear, word, understand, unfruitful, bear fruit, good soil,* etc.

b) *Relationships:* What is the relationship between hearing and understanding? What is the relationship between the things that hindered or helped in the growth and the results of the growth?

Focus on the illustration which you have been studying and ask yourself some additional questions which you feel need answering for a deeper understanding of this parable.

2. Interpret your questions.

a) USE CROSS-REFERENCES: Read Mark 4:14-20 and Luke 8:11-15. Note the additional information and the different ways the ideas are stated in these references. If you have studied one special illustration, focus on the verse which relates to your illustration.

b) COMPARE TRANSLATIONS: Read Matthew 13:18-23 and Luke 8:11-15 in some other translations to gain further insight.

c) DEFINE WORDS AND WRESTLE WITH MEANINGS: Think seriously about the meaning of some of the key words. What does it mean to *hear?* to *understand?* What is the relationship between *hearing* and *understanding? Not understanding?* What is the relationship of *understanding* and *good soil?* What is the meaning of *unfruitful?* To *bear fruit?*

Practice C — Personalize Biblical Teachings

In summarizing the teachings of this parable, it seems that Jesus was saying:

- There are at least four ways to respond to the Word of God.
- There are a variety of things which can hinder the response to and the growth of the Word in our hearts.
- There are a variety of outcomes.
- The degree of receptivity seems to determine the kind of response.

As we think in terms of how we might respond to these teachings, we might add to the summary:

- Any one of us can respond in one of these four ways at different times in our lives.
- There is a progression in the illustrations, from no response to a great deal of response. We all face many hindrances which can erode our faith, but the difference between the good soil and the other soils has to do with *perseverance, hanging on, holding fast.* The person with the good soil is one that holds fast to the promises of God no matter what are the problems or difficulties. Note that sin is not listed as one of the hindrances!

Ways to Apply and Actualize

1. Paraphrase the interpretation of this parable in terms of your own experiences.

2. Complete these statements:
   a) Learning how to study the Bible should help me in *understanding* . . .
   b) What I receive in this Bible study will depend on . . .
   c) Some hindrances which will prevent the Word of God growing in my life are . . .
   d) The Good News I find in this parable for me is . . .

3. Pray with your group on your individual responses to the Word.

CHAPTER **6**

Ways to Interpret

While you have already been involved in the process of interpretation in several discovery skills exercises, this chapter will describe the process in more detail.

Purpose of Interpretation

To interpret means to explain or tell the meaning of something. When interpreting a Scripture passage, your aim should be to determine what the author meant by the words which he used. You should try to put yourself in his place and recapture his thoughts, attitudes, and emotions. You should try to recreate in your mind the experiences of the author to discover why he wrote what he did in a certain historical situation for a specific purpose. Also you should try to understand the people for whom he was writing.

Please note that the primary purpose of interpretation is to discover what the *author meant* by what he said, to discover his purpose and message. This is not easy, because he is not around for us to ask him our questions. But we still should try to be objective in our interpretations. Thus, when we are trying to interpret, we are not to think about what the passage means to *us*, (this is *application*) but what it seemed to mean to the author. Even so, interpretations will vary a great deal. You can read a dozen commentaries on some biblical passage and have as many different explanations. Nor is it possible to know the meaning of everything in the Bible, because we lack the background or insight necessary for total understanding.

The Bridge Between Observation and Interpretation

Asking Questions for Understanding

As we have already stated, the bridge between observation and interpretation is to ask yourself *questions for understanding*, questions concerning the meaning of words and statements. This is a bridge we use more often than we realize. Usually when we read something, we automatically do three things: 1) We read the words in a passage; 2) we observe what the words are saying; 3) we ask ourselves questions about words and statements we do not understand. While we may do some of these things rather unconsciously in our general reading, in learning to become discoverers, we need to do these things deliberately. As we read a passage, we should force ourselves to ask questions about meanings.

Why Ask Questions?

Too often we read superficially and do not think seriously about what we are reading. We do not question ourselves about meanings of words, except those which really puzzle us. Because we are lazy in our thinking, we do not get much out of our reading.

Some of the reasons for asking questions are these: to stimulate our thinking; to force ourselves to think seriously about the meaning of words and statements; to begin to identify those words, phrases, and statements which need interpretation. Asking ourselves questions often will lead to more observations, prepare us for application, and serve as the foundation for questions which we might use in leading a discussion.

Learning to ask questions about meanings of words is a skill just like learning how to observe. At first persons do not know how to ask questions. One of the reasons is that they have never thought about asking questions. Another is that they may feel foolish about the kind they might ask, thinking that asking questions might reveal ignorance—and who wants to be considered ignorant!

One thing you need always remember is that you are asking *yourself* the questions for *your own understanding*. That is why we shall call these *questions for understanding*. They might also be called *interpretive* questions or *I wonder* questions (I wonder what is the meaning of . . . ?). These are not questions which you ask someone else. You are asking them to challenge yourself to think seriously about what you are reading and observing.

At first, you may see little sense in asking yourself questions. Especially, you may think it a waste of time to ask yourself questions about words and ideas whose meanings seem so apparent. But remember the purpose of asking questions. Recall your study of Matthew 6:25-34. You were to think about the meanings of such well-known words as *anxious, life, body*. Yet it was in the asking of questions that you were helped to discover their deeper meanings.

What Kind of Questions?

You have already been introduced to the kinds of questions to ask yourself. Now we shall consider them in greater detail, suggesting additional kinds of questions you might ask.

Remember that observing and asking questions should really be done simultaneously. You are to make your observations and ask your questions at the same time, but *do not stop* to answer any of your questions until you have completed your observations of the passage you are studying. Not until you have observed the whole passage are you ready to interpret any part of it. Don't cheat yourself of discoveries by jumping into interpretation too soon.

1. MEANING: What is the meaning of this word, phrase, statement? How can this word be defined? Is there a deeper meaning in the idea than appears on the surface?

2. SIGNIFICANCE: What is the significance of a key word, phrase, or statement in the passage? What is its importance to the message? What is the significance of the verb tenses, connectives, some of the grammatical constructions? What is the significance of some of the literary patterns, such as comparisons, contrasts, illustrations, repetitions, structure of passage? Why has the author used this particular term? Would it make any difference if this idea were left out? Or stated differently?

3. IMPLICATION: What is implied by the use of this term or phrase? What is implied by the use of a question, an illustration, etc.?

4. RELATIONSHIP: What is the relationship of words to other words? One part of a verse to another part? Verses to verses? Paragraphs with paragraphs? Chapters with chapters? Relationship of the beginning and end of a chapter or section?

5. PROGRESSION: Is there any progression in the thought pattern? Does it move toward a climax? Is one idea built on another? Is there any significance in the order of a series of words or ideas?

6. LITERAL OR FIGURATIVE: Is this term or statement to be considered literally or figuratively?

Overwhelming?

Do you feel overwhelmed with all of the ideas and suggestions for asking questions? Remember that this is just a list of possibilities. You will never ask all of these questions as you study a passage. At first, you may ask some irrelevant, but do not let that disturb you. As you seek to interpret a passage, you will soon learn to discern which of your questions are relevant and which are not.

When you first begin to ask yourself *questions for understanding,* you may mix application questions with the interpretive questions. Note the examples of some of the questions you might ask relating to Matthew 6:25.

- What is the meaning of *anxious?*
- What does Jesus mean by *life?*
- What is the significance of the illustrations—*what you shall eat— what you shall drink?*

- Why shouldn't we be anxious about life?
- Why shouldn't we be concerned about food and drink?

Note that the first three questions have to do with meanings. The last two have to do with application. While these application questions may come to your mind at the same time as you are thinking about meaning questions, you do not write these down. While you are focusing on the interpretation of a passage, you do not allow yourself to think about application. First, you are to discover what *Jesus meant* by his words. Then you can think about what they should mean to you.

Process of Interpretation

Let us recall that the purpose of interpretation is to discover what *the author meant* by what he said. The purpose of asking questions is to identify those areas which need interpretation. Not until you have carefully observed the details in a passage and asked yourself questions about the details are you ready to begin the process of interpreting. Never cheat yourself or the author by jumping into interpretation too soon. First *observe* what a passage really says. Then *interpret* what is said.

You have already been introduced to some of the approaches in the process of interpretation. Now we shall describe them in greater detail, listing them as steps, but they really do not have to be taken in the order listed.

Step One — PRAY and MEDITATE

Only with the guidance of the Holy Spirit can you interpret Scripture properly and receive insights into the truths. Prayer and meditation are first in the process of interpretation. Prayer is also important in the process of observation. Many a person has admitted that Bible study was only frustration until they seriously began to pray about their study. After you have observed the details in a passage and asked yourself questions, then take some time to meditate prayerfully and thoughtfully on some of the insights you discovered through the process. Give the Lord opportunity to be your Interpreter, to guide you in your thinking. An open heart, an open mind, and a spirit of receptivity are necessary characteristics of a Bible student.

Step Two — DISCERN

While prayer and meditation are important, you need also to use common sense and discernment when seeking to know meanings. The questions you have asked yourself reveal areas which need special thought and consideration, but you have to use discernment as to the validity of some of your questions. Some may overlap and some may be irrelevant. You will soon learn that a question which can be answered with *yes* or *no* does not have much value in the interpretive process. Also weed out any application question in which you have used the pronouns *we* or *me* or *us* (Why should *we* not be anxious?)

You are not to think of answering questions as an end in itself but as a means by which you gain deeper insight into the whole passage. You don't necessarily answer individual questions, but you use them as your guide when considering the meaning of a whole thought.

Step Three — DEFINE

The dictionary is one of the most important tools of the interpreter. Look up the definitions of the key words in the passage. Also note the synonyms given. Often new insights will come to you as you observe the many variations of meanings which can be applied to a word. Choose from the many definitions the one which best fits into the context of the Bible passage.

For deeper insight, study the etymology of a word—that is, its root significance and derivation in terms of origin and development through the centuries. To do this you need a good dictionary. Of course the best way to gain insight into meaning of words is to read a passage in the original Hebrew or Greek because some words are very difficult to translate into English.

When studying definitions be sure that you relate the definition to the Bible text. Always ask yourself, "What did the author have in mind when he used this word? What insight into the passage does this definition give me?" There is a tendency for some Bible students to look up definitions as an exercise without relating the definitions to the Bible text itself.

Step Four — COMPARE

Because of the difficulty scholars have in translating the Bible from the original Hebrew and Greek into English, it is always helpful to compare translations. Compare the standard versions such as *King James, American Standard, The New English Bible, The Jerusalem Bible,* and the *Revised Standard Version.* Also consult some of the more "free" translations and paraphrases such as *Phillips, Moffat,* the *Amplified Version, The Living Bible,* or *Good News for Modern Man.* Copy those portions which give you new insights into a passage.

Step Five — INVESTIGATE

Look for Scripture's own interpretations. Often in the Gospels, Jesus interprets his own statements by explanations and quotations from Old Testament. Use the marginal references and a concordance to find additional references relating to the word or concept which you are considering. You may find many more cross-references than you can use. Select only those which seem to broaden your understanding of the passage you are studying.

Step Six — CONSULT

Books in the Bible were written in a specific historical setting and were addressed to persons in concrete historical situations. The tendency of many of us is to read the Bible through twentieth-century eyes. We evaluate the customs and practices with our present day customs and practices. This is unfair to the writers of the Bible. Therefore, it is essential to consult other resources in order to gain insight into the historical, cultural, and geographical background of biblical days. We should try to understand the Bible through the eyes of those days. Thus we will not be as critical of some of the admonitions and standards set forth in the Bible. While these may not be like ours today, these customs or standards may reflect universal truths which are as applicable today as in that day.

Some of the resources to use are Bible dictionaries, Bible geographies, atlases. In the study of historical books, such as those found in the Old Testament and the Gospels and Acts in the New Testament, it is especially helpful to locate events on a map and study the customs and culture of that day. You can make an interesting Bible study by tracing the journeys of such Bible characters as Abraham, Jacob, David, Paul.

Because of the difficulty of many Bible passages, you may need to consult a commentary in order to comprehend the meaning, but this should be done *last*. If you consult a commentary before you have any individual study, you deny yourself the joy of discovering truths for yourself. Too many people are commentary students rather than Bible students. Use the commentary as a tool and not as a crutch.

Step Seven — WRESTLE

It is very possible to follow all of these steps and not come to any definite decisions in terms of the meaning of a verse or passage. You also have to wrestle with the information which you have gained. This means you have to think, meditate, evaluate, reflect, and draw conclusions. This leads you to the final step.

Step Eight — SUMMARIZE

The final step in the process of interpretation is to summarize your conclusions. You may need to summarize insights about individual words or verses as well as about an entire passage. A summary statement might begin with: "therefore, it seems that the *author* is saying . . . or means . . . " Always remember you are trying to interpret what the author meant by what he was saying.

46

Recording Your Interpretations

Purpose of Recording

While it is possible to interpret a passage and not write down your findings, you will gain much more in your study if you record your insights. Unless you write down what you discover, you might quickly forget your insights. Writing also forces you to be more exact in your analysis. Another purpose is to record your insights in such a way that you can share your findings more easily with others.

Ways to Record

One of the best ways is to record your findings chronologically according to verses. For instance, if you were recording insights gained in a study of Matthew 6:25-34, you might do the following things with 6:25:

1. List the definitions of key words in 6:25. Record only those definitions which fit in with the context of the passage.

2. Record phrases from some of the other translations which gave you new insight into 6:25.

3. List some of the cross-references you have found relating to the key ideas. You might copy one or two of the verses which give you special insight into the passage.

4. Record any significant information you gained from a Bible dictionary or commentary.

5. After wrestling with the information gained, then try to summarize what you learned.

Studying a Book

So far in your study, you have focused on several rather short and easy passages in order to learn some of the skills in observation and interpretation. Remember that one of the aims of this resource is to introduce these steps in Bible study slowly so that you will not become frustrated in the process. For persons who have not done much Bible study, frustration can lead to discouragement. I hope you have developed enough skill in observing and interpreting that you are ready for our next phase in this study, the Expanding Phase in which you study a book. You will continue to develop the techniques you have already learned, but new ones will be added.

We shall study the book of James because it is a short book and does not contain too many difficult theological problems. It is very practical in its approach. When you are developing skills, it is best not to become involved with difficult theological passages such as we find in some of Paul's letters. While your focus will be on the content in the book of James, the main purpose will be to perfect your skills in studying. You will not be able to analyze and interpret all that is in the book. But through the process, you will discover its main message and many of its teachings.

Observe the Whole Book

When you begin to study a book in the Bible, the first thing you should do is read the entire book quickly to get an overview of its contents. Then you study it by sections.

Each writer of a book in the Bible had a specific purpose for writing what he did. He had certain facts and truths which he desired to convey to his readers. His purpose determined the content of his book —which ideas and facts to include and which to omit. His purpose also determined the structure of his book—the way in which he arranged his material. Historical events and situations governed some of the content and approaches used by the author. His own personality and background influenced his literary style.

As you read through a book, here are some major things to observe:

PURPOSE: What is the author's purpose for writing this book?

CONTENT: What are the major truths and ideas which he is presenting in order to accomplish his purpose?

STRUCTURE: How has he arranged his material to emphasize his purpose?

LITERARY FORM: What literary forms does he use to bring out his message: prose, poetry, discourse, parable, drama, apocalyptic? When is the terminology literal and when figurative?

ATMOSPHERE: What is the underlying tone of the book? Or parts of the book?

Seek to Discover the Writer and His Purpose

As you read through a book the first time, focus on the writer and his purpose. Remember that he had a reason for writing what he did. He had some ideas, some experiences, or some convictions which he wanted others to know.

No book will carry a detailed description of the writer, but sometimes he will say things about himself, such as Paul often does in his epistles. You can gain insight into a writer's purpose and even into his personality by noting the things he emphasizes—his admonitions, his convictions, his concerns, his illustrations. He also reveals his purpose in the way he structures his book, the amount of space he gives to certain topics. This is especially true with the narrative books of the Old Testament, the Gospels and Acts in the New Testament. The writer of the book of Genesis uses 11 chapters to discuss beginnings and 39 chapters to discuss the story of a few persons. By the very structure of the book, one can assume that the purpose of the book of Genesis was to relate a story of a family and not the beginnings of mankind.

As you read, try to picture the person who wrote the book. Try to recreate in your mind what he had experienced or was experiencing at the time he was writing. What had he seen? What had he heard? What were his feelings and convictions which prompted him to write as he did?

Seek to Discover Facts About the Readers

In some instances, the biblical writers had specific readers in mind. This is especially true of the New Testament epistles. As you read a book the first time, try to discover the kind of persons to whom the author was writing. What seemed to be their problems and characteristics? Sometimes the writer specifically states the problems, and sometimes he implies their problems by the things he emphasizes and the admonitions he gives. Try to identify with these persons who would receive this letter. How would you feel as you read or heard someone else read this letter? In order to identify with the persons, you may need to know more about the historical background and culture of their times.

Observe the Structure of the Book

Also in your first reading, see if you can discover something about the structure of the book. You may have difficulty doing this. Some books do not have as definite a structure as others. But keep on the alert for the way the chapters are grouped together according to content. Usually in the epistles the first chapters focus on doctrine and the last ones on practical living.

There are a variety of ways a writer can organize his material. Note the following list. A book may reflect several of the kinds.

BIOGRAPHICAL: in terms of the lives of people. The Book of Genesis is an example in which the material is organized according to the lives of Abraham, Isaac, Jacob, and Joseph.

HISTORICAL: in terms of succession of events. The Book of Exodus is an example in which the material is organized according to the experiences of the Children of Israel as they traveled from Egypt to the Land of Canaan.

CHRONOLOGICAL: in terms of the time when events happened. Both Genesis and Exodus are also examples of this type of organization in that the story is told in chronological order.

GEOGRAPHICAL: in terms of the places where the events happened. The Book of Exodus is also geographical in arrangement in that the places as well as the events are emphasized.

LOGICAL OR IDEOLOGICAL: in terms of the ideas themselves. The prophetical books and the epistles are examples of these types of arrangements. The Book of Romans is logical in structure, whereas the Book of Philippians is ideological, organized according to ideas but not in logical sequence.

Focus on Smaller Sections

After you have read the entire book, begin to focus on one section at a time. Usually you begin with the first paragraph of the first chapter. But wherever you begin, it is important that you see the section in the context of the whole book. That is the reason for reading the entire book first, even though you read it very quickly. Then you are able to analyze the one section in the context of the entire book.

For these suggestions to have value, you need to begin to practice them with the book of James.

Practice A — Read the Book of James

1. Observe the writer and readers.

Before you begin to read the book of James, divide a sheet of paper in half. Entitle the left half of the sheet, *The author: his characteristics, convictions, and concerns.* Entitle the right half, *The readers: their characteristics, problems, concerns.*

As you read, jot down things you learn about the author and his readers from what the author says and the things he emphasizes. Don't go into too much detail. Write down some of the obvious things. This is your first time through the book, and you are to gain just a brief look at the author and readers. If there are several of you in your study group, you might divide the chapters. All of you should read the entire book, but each would be responsible for one chapter in terms of what you learned about author and readers. Afterwards, you are to share with each other what you discovered in your first reading.

2. Summarize purpose.

After this first reading, try to summarize in a few statements what you think is the author's purpose for writing this book.

3. Consider the structure of James.

The book of James is not written in a logical order such as Paul writes many of his epistles. There seems to be no pattern, just a series of ideas like beads on a string. Someone has said that the book of James was more like a sermon, the kind that was preached in his day. Some scholars suggest that it might first have been a sermon and later put into writing. It has the quality of a spoken sermon. As you read the book, you can sense the changes in the mood of the "preacher" from pleadings to stern admonitions. Sometimes you can almost imagine him shaking his first at his audience as he reprimands them for some of the things they have been doing.

4. Consider the author.

There are varying opinions as to the identity of the author of the book of James. Some claim he was the brother of Jesus. Others say he was one of the apostles. Read in a commentary or Bible dictionary the various views as to the authorship of James.

Practice B — Observe Details of James 3:6-12

1. Review.

You have already had several practices in observing the details in passages. You are to continue to develop these skills in this practice.

In our study of the book of James, we shall begin with one of the paragraphs in the center of the book, James 3:6-12. We begin with this paragraph because it is an easy one to analyze. It focuses on only a few concepts.

In your previous studies, you were introduced gradually to some of the techniques of observation. Usually you were directed as to what to look for. Now you are to put into practice all the things you have been learning about observation. Review the suggestions on how to observe—the short list in Chapter 3 and the more detailed in Chapter 4.

In order to help you review the ways to observe, we shall describe in detail how you might begin your study of this section.

2. Read thoughtfully.

As you begin to study this passage, you should read it prayerfully and thoughtfully—praying that the Holy Spirit would guide you in your reading and thoughtfully noting the words of the passage. Let us consider the first verse and the way you might think about it as you read.

"And the tongue is a fire. The tongue is an unrighteous world among our members, staining the whole body, setting on fire the cycle of nature, and set on fire by hell" 3:6.

As you read the words in the first sentence, you note that the key words are *tongue* and *fire*. You note that this is a comparison, the tongue is called a fire. Also you note that the verb is present tense. As you make note of these things, you might begin asking yourself some questions: "Why does he call the tongue *a fire?* Any significance in the present-tense verb?" As you read on, you note that he calls the tongue something else: *an unrighteous world.* Again you might say to yourself, "What does he mean by that phrase?" Reading on, you note other statements describing the tongue, words and phrases about which you may wonder, such as *staining, cycle of nature, set on fire by hell.*

As we have said before, this process of wondering about the meanings of words and phrases is a natural process of the mind. When a person begins to think about a portion of writing, the normal action of the mind is to observe key words and phrases and begin to question meanings. Bible students have often stopped at that point, just as the mind was beginning to function. They may see so many terms they do not understand that they close their Bibles and say, "What's the use?" But the process of questioning reveals that the mind is warming up to enable the student to find solutions to his questions. Remember that the questions you are asking yourself are *I wonder questions* or *questions for understanding.*

3. Observe and record deliberately.

You can continue to study this section of James, observing words and phrases and wondering about meanings in a hit-and-miss fashion, or you can proceed in a logical and deliberate pattern, disciplining yourself to concentrate on the words you observe and to ask questions for understanding. The best way to study is to record your observations and questions on paper.

Take a sheet of paper and divide it into three equal sections. Use your paper horizontally so as to get sections as wide as possible. Entitle your sections as follows:

Observations	Scripture Passage	Questions for Understanding

In the *center section* write down portions of the Scripture passage in sequence. It is best to copy parts of a verse at a time, rather than a whole verse, but always include a unit of words such as a phrase or clause which has a unified idea. Note how the Bible passages are arranged on page 54.

In the *left section* record your observations. In the *right section* record the questions which you ask yourself about meanings. Remember that the purpose for asking yourself questions is to help yourself note the areas which may need special interpretation. You are trying to determine what the author meant by his words.

Note the *Example* on page 54. When recording observations, it is sometimes helpful to underline words and phrases taken from Scripture. The words which would be underlined are in italics. You will note that in the example, the observations are much more detailed than you have previously done. Now you are being encouraged to be more detailed in your observations. At first, you may have difficulties in knowing what to say about words and phrases, but practice will develop your powers of observation. The example focuses on 3:6-8. You continue with 3:9-12.

Practice C — Seek to Know Meanings

1. Select some key questions

After making a thorough study of James 3:6-12, you may have asked many more questions than you may have time to answer—or are even relevant to the message of the passage. Select just a few which you feel are relevant to understanding the passage. If there are several in your study group, each of you can take one verse and make a more thorough interpretation of it.

2. Interpret some of your questions

Review Chapter 6 on interpretation, especially the section on how to record interpretations (page 47). Follow those suggestions as you seek to interpret some of the words or statements in this passage.

Example

Observations	Scripture Passage	Questions for Understanding
6. *tongue* and *fire*—key words. comparison—tongue with fire. *is*—present tense verb second comparison—*tongue* with *world*; *un-righteous* describes the kind of world; *among our members* describes place. *staining*—shows action of tongue. *whole*—describes the extent of influence of body. *setting*—another action of tongue. *cycle of nature*—describes what is set on fire. Note change in verb—*set*, past tense; the tongue is acted upon. It sets things on fire and is set on fire—reveals source of fire.	James 3:6 And the tongue is a fire. The tongue is an unrighteous world among our members. staining the whole body, setting on fire the cycle of nature and set on fire by hell.	Meaning of *tongue?* Why is the tongue called a fire? Does the present tense verb imply tongue always is a fire? Why didn't James say "like a fire"? Would meaning be the same? Meaning of *unrighteous world?* Meaning of *among our members?* Significance of word *staining?* How can the tongue stain the whole body? Meaning of Body? Meaning of *cycle of nature?* How can the tongue influence the cycle of nature? Significance of this statement? Does James really mean that the tongue is set on fire by hell?
7. *for*—key connective, implies a reason. Introduces an illustration. *every kind*—all inclusive, all kinds of animals mentioned. *can be tamed*—implies possibilities. *has been tamed*—describes what has happened in past. 8. *but*—key connective, brings out contrast as to what man can do with animals, even savage ones, but not with his tongue. Again emphasis on word *tame.* Note descriptive words about tongue, words which can be used to describe animals.	For every kind of beast and bird or reptile and sea creature can be tamed and has been tamed by humankind. 8. *but* no human being can tame the tongue— a restless evil, full of deadly poison.	Why this illustration? Why such an all inclusive statement? Meaning of word *tame?* Significance of word *humankind?* Significance of word *human being?* Does this imply that God can do what mankind cannot do? Significance of these descriptive words? Relationship of verses 7 and 8 with verse 6?

As reminders, here are some things to do:

a) STATE YOUR QUESTION.

b) DEFINE SOME KEY WORD.

c) READ TRANSLATIONS: record parts of the translation which give you insight into meanings.

d) LOOK UP SEVERAL CROSS-REFERENCES. Copy down those verses which seem to provide additional insight.

f) STUDY OTHER RESOURCES. Possibly, you will need to read a commentary to see what is meant by some of the statements.

g) WRESTLE WITH MEANINGS AND SUMMARIZE. Do some personal wrestling with what you have been learning through these processes and formulate a statement summarizing what you think the author means by what he was saying.

Practice D – Personalize Biblical Teachings

We can all easily identify with some of the things which James says about the tongue. We have experienced its power to *burn* and *destroy* but also its power to *bless, affirm,* and *encourage.* Consider ways in which you might personalize the truths in this passage.

Evaluation

Is this description of the tongue a true description? What is the significance of the present tenses of the verbs? Do we always have the power to choose what our tongues will do?

Application

Complete some of these statements:

a) One time when I experienced the power of the tongue to *bless* or to *burn* . . .

b) One time when I learned how the use of my tongue can "defile my body" . . .

c) The greatest difficulty I have with my tongue is . . .

Actualization

a) Discuss how the use of your tongue can help or hinder the relationships in your study group.

b) Use your tongue to *bless* by sharing with the other members one thing you admire about each one.

c) Share any problems you may have with your tongue and invite the others to pray with you about the use of your tongue.

Practice A — Observe and Record Details

After you have completed a study of James 3:6-12, then do a similar study of James 3:1-5. Divide a sheet of paper in three sections as you did for 3:6-12. Entitle your sections as follows:

Observations	Scripture Passage	Questions for Understanding

In the center section, copy units of thought from James 3:1. Record your observations in the left section and your questions about meanings in the right section. In this passage note the admonitions, warnings, reasons for doing things, conditional clause and results, illustrations, comparisons, emphatic statements. Also note carefully the verb tenses.

If there are several in your group, you might divide the verses: James 3:1-3; 4-5 or James 3:1-2, 3-4; 5. It is best if several can work on the same verses so that there can be greater sharing of insights.

Practice B — Seek to Know Meanings

Try to interpret the verses which you observed, following the same pattern you used in the study of James 3:6-12. Record your findings.

1. Select some of your key questions.
2. Define some of the key words.
3. Compare translations.
4. Study cross-references, noting especially Luke 6:43-45.
5. Consult some resources to learn more about the position of *teachers* in the days of James.
6. Wrestle with the meanings of some of the comparisons made and summarize your conclusions.

Practice C — Personalize Biblical Teachings

You need to consider James 3:1-5 and 6-12 together because they really are a unified thought. James' emphasis is on the serious responsibility of being a teacher. In that day Christianity was in its infancy and was spread through teaching. No doubt there were many who wanted to be known as the "teachers of faith," some who may not have been very sincere in their motives. James is warning them about the dangers of being a teacher, because they are subject to greater judgment from both God and men. The tongue is a vehicle of communication but a dangerous member of our body which can do more damage than any other part of the body if it is not controlled.

Evaluation

Consider what James is saying about the tongue and persons in leadership. How do you react to the following statements:

1. Persons in leadership are subject to greater judgment and criticism;
2. If a person can control his tongue, he can control his whole body.

Application

How would you apply Luke 6:43-45 to James 3:1-5? How can our tongues be controlled?

Creative Expression

Meditate on the insights you have gained through this study on the tongue (James 3:1-12). Reflect one of your insights in some creative way: make a poster illustration; make a montage of pictures; write a poem, song, prayer, or devotional; or something else that you would like to do. You may do this individually or with several of your group members. Share what you do with the rest of the members.

CHAPTER 8

Observing the Whole

One real danger in Bible study is to get lost in the single phrases and verses of a Bible passage and never understand the entire message the author was trying to communicate. This is a special danger when using the skills which we have been discussing in our previous chapters. We must beware of observing words and phrases as ends in themselves, no matter how interesting or meaningful they are. We need to observe the words and phrases in relation to the whole sentence, the whole paragraph, the whole chapter. We study the parts of a passage in order to understand the main message of a chapter or book; otherwise we will not grasp fully what the author was trying to communicate.

In order to understand the whole we need to learn how to analyze the structure of a scriptural passage—the way in which the author has arranged his material.

Definition of Structure

The term "structure" refers to the underlying design, framework, skeleton, organization, or arrangement of material. Anything that is planned with a specific purpose will have structure, whether it is a building, a car, a piece of music, a watch, or literary composition. The function of a thing determines its form. Insight into the design and structure of a production helps a person better understand the purpose of the production.

We might compare this process of observing the structure of a passage to observing a new house. Let us imagine that I invited you out to see my new house. When we arrived, scattered all over the yard were various parts that would make a house. There were window frames and windows, the doors, the walls, and the bricks. Were I to say to you, "Here is my house," no doubt you would reply, "I see the parts that make up a house, but I still don't know what your house looks like."

So it is in Bible study. It is not enough just to see the parts, or even understand the parts. You need to see the parts in relation to the whole before you can grasp the entire message.

As you read a passage in the Bible, you may not be conscious that it has any structure. If you are reading in the King James version, you are conscious only of individual verses. But if you are reading in some other versions, you may be conscious of the paragraphs, but still not think that there is a structure in the paragraph. Possibly you are asking, "How does a person observe structure of a paragraph?"

Observing Structure Through a Diagram

One of the best ways to analyze a passage is to make a structural diagram of it. Copy on a sheet of paper all of the words in a paragraph, but arrange the units of thought in as graphic way as possible. In chapters 3 and 4 there are examples of structural diagrams of Matthew 6:25-34 and 1 Corinthians 13. Review these as you consider the following suggestions. To make a structural diagram, here are some of the things you do:

1. Copy down the units of phrases and clauses in the center of a page, separating the units so that they have the most meaning to you.

2. Line up major clauses and ideas so that the key ideas can most easily be seen.

3. Place modifying phrases and clauses under the words which they describe. Do not do this to the extent that you break up the thought pattern too much.

4. Place series of words, phrases, clauses, parallel thoughts, and parallel constructions under one another.

Value of Structural Diagram

Possibly these suggestions sound confusing to you, but this too is a skill you learn through practice. There is no right or wrong way to set up a structural diagram. Any way that makes sense to you will have value. The very process of doing it will enable you to gain deeper insight into the passage. This is especially true if you are studying a very difficult passage. When once you get the ideas in front of you in some graphic form, it is easier to see the key ideas and relationships of the parts to the whole.

How to Analyze Your Structural Diagram

After you have arranged the units of thought of a passage in a graphic way on a page, then try to analyze its contents by doing some of these things:

1. Study your verses and bracket those which seem to be on the same topic.

2. Summarize the main thought or emphasis in each group of verses and write your summary in the left margin. Try to summarize using just a phrase or sometimes even one word.

3. Identify key words and ideas by underlining and circling them. You might want to use colored pencils to highlight ideas. Circle key connectives.

4. Use arrows and lines to show relationships, repeated words, and other things you observe.

5. In the left margin, record your other observations—noting commands, warnings, conditional clauses, reasons and results, comparisons, contrasts, and grammatical constructions.

6. In the right margin, list some of your *questions for understanding,* based on your observations.

Practice A — Consider Diagrams

1. Analyze diagrams.

On page 62 there is a structural diagram of James 3:1-12. Note how the diagram is constructed. Were you to diagram the passage, you might want to arrange the unit of thoughts differently, but this gives you an example of one way to do them.

Study the diagram and bracket the verses which seem closely related in emphasis. In the left margin summarize each grouping in a brief statement.

2. Make a structural diagram.

Read James 3:13-18 and make a structural diagram of this paragraph. Follow the suggestions on page 59. Make your diagram in the center of the page, allowing margins. Try to get the entire diagram on one page; type, if possible. If you place your diagram in the center of a sheet, crosswise, you will have more margin space. You may have to use two sheets.

3. Analyze diagram.

Bracket those verses which seem to focus on one idea. Summarize each grouping in a brief statement.

Using a colored pencil, underline and circle key words, connectives, and ideas. In the left margin, record what you observe, noting admonitions, contrasts, conditional clauses, descriptive words, and series of ideas. In the right margin, list your questions for understanding.

Practice B — Seek to Know Meanings

Try to interpret verses which you have observed in James 3:13-18, following the pattern which you have been using in your previous studies. Record your findings.

1. Select one or two of your key questions.
2. Define some of the key words, especially the term *wisdom*.
3. Compare translations.
4. Study cross-references, especially some relating to wisdom.
5. Consult resources. If you do not have many resource books, assign one or two persons in your group to be the resource experts. They would be responsible for supplying information concerning the entire passage.
6. Wrestle with information which you gained in your study. Summarize your conclusions in some brief statements.

1. Let not many of you become teachers, my brethren,
   for you know that we who teach
     shall be judged with greater strictness.

2. For we all make many mistakes,
   and if any one makes no mistakes
       in what he says
   he is a perfect man,
       able to bridle the whole body also.

3. If we put bits into the mouths of horses
           that they may obey us,
   we guide their whole bodies.

4. Look at the ships also;
     though they are so great
     and are driven by strong winds,
   they are guided by a very small rudder
     wherever the will of the pilot directs.

5. So the tongue is a little member
     and boasts of great things.
   How great a forest is set ablaze by a small fire!

6. And the tongue is a fire.
   The tongue is an unrighteous world,
                 among our members,
     staining the whole body,
     setting on fire the cycle of nature,
     and is set on fire by hell.

7. For every kind of beast and bird,
           of reptile and sea creature,
   can be tamed and
   has been tamed by humankind,

8. but no human being
     can tame the tongue—
       a restless evil, full of deadly poison.

9. With it we bless the Lord and Father,
     and with it we curse men,
       who are made in the likeness of God.

10. From the same mouth
      come blessing and cursing.
    My brethren, this ought not to be so.

11. Does a spring pour forth
      from the same opening fresh water and brackish?

12. Can a fig tree, my brethren, yield olives,
      or a grapevine figs?
    No more can salt water yield fresh.

Practice C — Personalize Biblical Teachings

Now that you have studied the entire Chapter 3 of James, you should consider the relationship of the three paragraphs with each other. In terms of key words, the paragraphs might be summarized in three words: *teachers, tongue, wisdom.* But you might ask, why this emphasis on *wisdom?*

Remember that in the days of James there was great emphasis on teaching. But there was also great emphasis on *wisdom.* Possibly there were many teachers who were proud and boastful about their wisdom —their knowledge about the Christian faith. It seems that James is warning them about the dangers of being a teacher because of their greater responsibility, but if they really are interested in being known as wise teachers, they must demonstrate this wisdom. True wisdom is revealed more through actions than through words. He seems to be saying, "If any of you wants to be known as wise and understanding, demonstrate your wisdom in a life of gentleness, humility, graciousness, and peace." If they preach a gospel of love and don't reveal it through their actions, they are preaching a lie.

Evaluation

How would you compare James 3:13-18 and 1 Corinthians 13?

Application and Actualization

Reflect on some of the following suggestions:

1. Meditate on James 3:17-18. How might the statements in these verses be a pattern for demonstrating "true wisdom" in your Bible study group? In your home relationships? Describe specific examples.
2. Complete the statements:
    a) When trying to demonstrate "true wisdom," my greatest problem is . . .
    b) Some Good News I find in James 3 is . . .
3. Share with your group members an area in which you feel you need more wisdom. Pray with one another concerning your needs.

CHAPTER 9

Summarizing Through Charts

In your study you have been analyzing smaller biblical sections in order to learn the skills of study. You have been involved a great deal in the skills of observation because these are very important skills to learn in Bible study. The more proficient you become in observing a passage, the richer will be your interpretations and applications.

So far in your study, you have been writing down every word in a paragraph and focusing on as many details as possible. But when you study longer sections of scripture, it is not always possible to copy down every word in a passage. This is too time-consuming. You have to learn how to abbreviate the process. One of the best ways is through the use of charts. When you are analyzing a chapter, instead of copying down every word, you can summarize the key ideas on a horizontal or vertical chart.

Horizontal Chart

In making a horizontal chart, construct your chart lengthwise on a sheet of paper. *(Note example on page 66.)* Draw a line across the page. Block off as many divisions, both above and below the main line as you have paragraphs in a chapter. Your divisions might even be in proportion to the size of your paragraphs, with more space for the longer paragraphs and less for the shorter ones.

Title your paragraphs according to the content. Place your titles above the main line. In the sections below the line, list the main ideas found in each paragraph. Bracket the paragraphs which seem to be on the same topic.

Vertical Chart

This type of chart is constructed vertically on a sheet of paper. *(Note example on page 66.)* Draw a large rectangle and block out the divisions according to the paragraphs. Vertical charts are best for shorter portions of material or for a chapter in which there are not too many paragraphs. If a chapter has many paragraphs, the horizontal is better to use. The vertical chart is very good to use when you want to study the relationship of ideas within paragraphs and between paragraphs. Again you bracket paragraphs which seem to focus on the same ideas and record summary titles in the margins outside the chart.

Value of Charts

Charting a passage has its particular value for these reasons:

1. Forces you to think graphically about the material in a passage.
2. Helps you see the major ideas.
3. Helps you see relationships between paragraphs.
4. Helps you identify ideas which are emphasized in more than one paragraph—ideas which may be repeated or emphasized in a variety of ways.
5. Helps you to summarize ideas.
6. Helps you see everything in context. Once you have charted a chapter, you can make a more thorough study of just those sections which you choose, but you will always be studying the section in context with the whole chapter.

Practice A — Summarize with Charts

Since you have already studied the different paragraphs in James 3, summarize the teachings in this chapter with a vertical chart. Draw a rectangle in the center of a sheet of paper. Divide the rectangle into three sections according to the paragraphs.

List the major ideas in each paragraph.

Place in the left margin a summary title for each paragraph. Try to indicate the relationship between the paragraphs. What is the relationship between the paragraph on teachers, the one on the tongue and the one on wisdom?

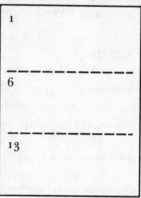

Practice B — Make a Horizontal Chart of James 1

1. Read chapter one in James.

There are two ways to set up a horizontal chart for this chapter. One is to construct it according to paragraphs. The other is to construct it according to the main divisions.

ACCORDING TO PARAGRAPHS: This is the kind of chart you have to make when you first read a chapter. Until you study the chapter, you do not know what might be the main divisions. But one of the problems of this kind of chart is that the spaces may become so small you are limited in your recording.

Chart of James 1 according to paragraphs:

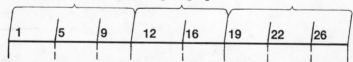

ACCORDING TO MAJOR DIVISIONS: In this type of chart the paragraphs are listed under the main divisions and you have more space in which to record. Note the sample.

Chart of James 1 according to divisions:

1	5	9	12	16	19	22	26
1- 2-4 5-8 9-11			12-15 16-18		19-21 22-25 26-27		

2. Title your paragraphs according to their content.

Place your titles in the spaces above the line. In the sections below the line, summarize the main ideas in each paragraph. Note the admonitions, reasons, results, and promises. If there are several in your group, you might divide the paragraphs, each focusing on one or two.

Example of how to summarize James 1:1-4:

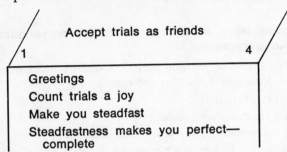

Accept trials as friends

1   4

Greetings
Count trials a joy
Make you steadfast
Steadfastness makes you perfect—
    complete

3. Bracket those paragraphs which seem to be on the same topic.

In order to help you, grouping has been suggested in the charts. Here are some possible titles for the groupings:

James 1:1-11   Admonitions relating to trials
James 1:12-18   Admonitions relating to temptations
James 1:19-27   Admonitions relating to the Word

Practice C — Study One Paragraph

After you have made a summary chart of James 1, showing an overview of the major teachings, then you need to study each paragraph more thoroughly. For practice you are to concentrate on just one paragraph. If there are several in your group, each of you are to select one paragraph for special study. You are to make a thorough study of this paragraph, using the skills which you have been learning. Then afterwards, share with one another the insights gained.

Here are the steps to follow:

1. Select one paragraph.

2. Observe its contents.

Follow the pattern which you have been using.

Observations	Scripture	Questions for Understanding
	(Make a structural diagram such as you made with James 3:13-18. If you can't get it all on one page, use two pages.)	

3. Select a few of your key questions for interpretation.

Follow the process which you have been using when interpreting statements in a passage: define words; compare translations; look up one or two cross references; wrestle with meanings; summarize. Some of the statements in this chapter are difficult to interpret, and you may need to study a commentary to get someone else's insight.

4. Consider some ways in which you might personalize the truths in your paragraph.

Think how you might apply and actualize one of the truths in a real-life situation. You might use this pattern:

    a) One thing I can believe is . . .
    b) One thing I am encouraged to do . . .
    c) One thing this passage teaches about relationships is . . .
    d) The Good News I find in this passage which meets one of my needs is . . .

CHAPTER 10

More About Interpretation

In every passage you have studied so far, you have been involved in some interpretation. You have practiced the different ways a person can gain insight into meanings of a passage. You have no doubt varied in the thoroughness in your study. Depth in interpreting a passage depends a great deal on the time you invest and the availability of resources. One of the first and very important aspects of interpretation is the study of key words in the passage. In this chapter we shall focus in detail on the things you might do in the study of key words.

Use of Dictionary

The dictionary is one of the most important tools a biblical discoverer needs to learn how to use. Here are some of the uses of the dictionary.

DEFINITIONS: The most common use of the dictionary is to study the definitions of a word. Usually there are several from which to choose, and you must select those which best fit in with the context of the passage.

SYNONYMS: Also study the synonyms given for a particular word. Here again you must select those which best fit into the context of the passage. Sometimes it is helpful to look up the definitions of some of the synonyms in order to gain as clear an understanding of a key word as possible. Even studying some of the antonyms can be helpful.

EXAMPLES: In larger dictionaries, often there are examples of the usage of a word. Many times you can find an example relating to a religious or theological use. These too can add insight into meanings.

ETYMOLOGY OF WORD: This is the study of word origins and development through the centuries. Most larger dictionaries include etymology of a word, usually in brackets after the pronunciation of the word. To understand the etymology of a word, you need to learn some of the simple abbreviations and symbols, such as ME for Middle English, AS for Anglo-Saxon, FR for French, G for German, GR for Greek. The word that comes first within the brackets is usually the most recent form of the word.

Use of Translations

As you seek to interpret a passage, you must always be mindful that an English version is always one step removed from the original language of Hebrew or Greek. In many cases it has been very difficult for translators to find English words which mean the same as the word used in the original Hebrew or Greek. Therefore, the best way to find the true definition of a word is to read a passage in the original. Since many of us cannot read Hebrew or Greek, we need other resources to help us.

Because scholars do have this difficulty of translating words from the original language into English, it is necessary to read a passage in several translations to see the various ways a word can be translated. There are some translations, such as the *Amplified Version* of the Bible, which provide a variety of ways a word might be translated.

Use of Cross-References

As you may have found already, you can gain insight into meaning of words by studying other cross-references in which the word is used. With the use of a concordance, you can find many references to a word. You select only those which fit into the context of your passage.

Use of Other Resources

Sometimes you do need the help of other scholars in order to understand a word, such help as you can find in a Bible dictionary, or a commentary. A very helpful book for word study is Alan Richardson, *A Theological Word Book of the Bible.* He supplies definitions and background information for many of the key words in the Bible.

Practice A — Be on the Alert for Details

1. Study James 2:1-7.

Remember that as you observe a passage, always be alert as to what you can learn about the author and readers. As you read these verses, focus on the writer and the readers and what you learn about them.

- Try to imagine what the author was *seeing, hearing, feeling* as he wrote these words. Select words which reveal feelings.
- Note the use of questions and how he answers them.
- Note the contrasts.

2. Study James 2:8-13.

- Underline what you consider are some of the key words.
- Note all of the conditional clauses and the results suggested.
- Note the admonitions and warnings.

3. Study James 2:14-26.

- Underline what seem to be some of the key words.
- Count how many times *faith* and *works* is used.
- Note use of questions and how they are answered.

Practice B — Seek to Know Meanings

1. Study key words.

This chapter in James has sometimes been the focus of controversy. Because of what James says, Luther felt that the book should not be included in the Bible. He felt that Paul and James did not agree in their interpretation of *faith* and *works*.

There are many things that need interpretation in this chapter, such as the relationship of the rich and the poor in 2:1-7; the meaning of the words *law, royal law, whole law, law of liberty* in 2:8-13. If you have the time, focus on these passages also, but I am suggesting that you concentrate mainly on the key words in James 2:14-26: *faith, works, believe, justified.* Since the emphasis in this chapter is on word study, make a study of these words. Here are the things to do:

- Define the words through use of dictionary;
- Study other translations;
- Study some cross references, such as Ephesians 2:8-10.

2. Summarize insights in a visual way.

You might summarize your insights in a paragraph, but instead try to express your insights in a visual way. Try to illustrate your concept of the relationship between *faith* and *works* through a poster, diagram, illustration, or picture, using symbols, words, pictures, circles, squares, lines, colors—anything that will enable you to express visually your concept of what James is saying.

If there are several in your group, work together in groups of two, three or four and make an illustration on a large sheet of paper.

CHAPTER 11

More About Charts and Summarization

In previous chapters we have discussed the importance of observing the way an author has arranged his material as well as observing what he said. Until you have insight into both content and structure of the biblical material, you really cannot fully understand the author's purpose for writing. A summary should reveal both content and arrangement of the Bible passage.

Importance of Summarization

Summaries help crystallize major teachings and are an aid to the memory. Always keep the parts related to the whole:

Relate verses to the whole paragraph
Relate paragraphs to the whole chapter
Relate chapters to the whole book
Relate individual truths to the whole message

In previous chapters we have focused on the use of structural diagrams and charts in order to analyze material and summarize content. In this chapter we shall review and enlarge on the subject of the use of charts, outlines, and diagrams in Bible study.

General Ways to Summarize

1. BOOK CHART: When studying a book, make a horizontal chart, blocking off a space for each chapter. Give a title to each chapter. Group the chapters into divisions according to similarity in content. Title the divisions. List the main teachings and the main characteristics of the book.

2. CHAPTER CHART: When studying a chapter, make a horizontal or vertical chart for each chapter, allowing space for each paragraph. Give each paragraph a factual or interpretive title. List the main teachings in each paragraph. Group the paragraphs according to their similarity in emphasis.

3. PARAGRAPH CHART: Chart or diagram the main teachings in any paragraph which demands special study.

4. TOPICAL CHART: If your Bible study is topical, make a chart to show the various aspects of your topic. For example, if you were considering the topic of prayer, you might chart your findings under these headings: *prayer admonitions; prayer promises; conditions for answered prayers.*

5. OUTLINE: List the main and subordinate points in a logical or topical outline. While outlines have their value, they are not as visual as a chart.

6. BRIEF STATEMENT: Summarize the author's purpose or the content of a paragraph or chapter in a brief phrase or statement.

7. PARAPHRASE: Write the content of a paragraph in your own words. Follow the text, but try to paraphrase it with the language of today.

8. SUMMARY DIAGRAM: Try to show relationship of ideas in a visual way.

Summary Diagrams

The term *diagram* may cause confusion in your mind since we have used it previously in our discussion on ways to observe structure of a paragraph. We used the term *structural diagram* when describing a way to arrange the units of thought in a paragraph so that you could more easily observe the structure and content of the paragraph.

A *summary diagram* is an arrangement of ideas to show their relationship to each other. In the *structural diagram* you wrote down all of the words in a paragraph. In a *summary diagram* you list only the principal ideas which you are seeking to analyze. It differs from an outline in that it is more informal. It differs from a chart in that it is not boxed by lines.

Reread James 1:26-27. The content of these verses can better be understood if the ideas are analyzed according to their relationships. The summary diagram is a simple way to place the truths of a passage in a graphic form.

Theme: Tests of religion

Description of person		Test	Situation	Results
		Bridles not his tongue	Deceives self	vain religion
Thinks himself religious	*Possibilities*			
		Visits poor Keeps self unstained	Honest with self and God	Pure religion

Summary diagrams may be done in visual and graphic ways using other things besides words, such as symbols, lines, circles, arrows, or squares. The purpose is to try to set before yourself in a graphic and visual way the key teachings of a verse or passage so that you can better understand its teachings. In Chapter 10, page 71, you were encouraged to make a visual diagram to show the relationship between *faith* and *works*.

Summarization by Means of Charts

The chart is one of the most effective ways to enable you to grasp the whole picture of a chapter or book. It has real value as a study device and equal value as a teaching tool. As we have stated before, charts can be horizontal or vertical. The purpose of a chart is to block out the contents of a paragraph, chapter or book in such a way that both content and relationships can be more easily seen and understood.

STUDY CHART   The purpose of a study chart is to record in graphic form the observations you make as you study some portion of Scripture. Your study chart can be as involved as you desire to make it. For example, as you study some chapter, you may want to trace what each paragraph teaches about certain ideas. You would make a horizontal chart, blocking off as many sections as paragraphs. As you concentrate on each paragraph you could list the major teachings, concepts of God, attitudes toward God, or key phrases. Even though you may find many things you would like to record, limit your chart to one or two pages. A chart loses its value if it covers too many pages.

SUMMARY CHART   Whereas your study chart may be very detailed, your summary chart should be simple and concise. From your study chart, you sift out most of the details and keep only the key ideas. The purpose of the summary chart is to set before yourself a bird's eye view of the principal teachings in a passage. Whereas your study chart can be factual in nature, your summary chart might be factual or interpretive.

TEACHING CHART   A teaching chart is the chart which you place on a chalkboard in order to help your students gain insight into the key ideas in a passage. Your summary chart may also serve as your teaching chart. It is best if you gradually develop your teaching chart as you discuss each idea. If possible you should encourage your students to help you develop the teaching chart. You will include whatever is necessary to convey the message and structure of a passage.

What to Include in a Chart

1. Main divisions of a chapter or book
2. Theme, titles of paragraphs or chapters
3. Key words, phrases, key ideas, verses
4. Relationships: comparisons, contrasts, repetitions, cause and effect, progression of ideas
5. Perspective: relationship of chapters
6. Proportion: amount of space given to major topics
7. Arrangement of material: geographical, biographical, chronological, psychological, ideological
8. Characteristics of chapters and books
9. Topical studies: teachings about God, man, sin, redemption
10. Literary features: quotable passages, figures of speech

What to Consider When Making a Chart

1. Make your chart so that ideas can be seen at a glance.
2. Avoid making it too large or too involved. If you have much information which you desire to chart, break it down into several charts.
3. Try to condense your information into words and phrases.
4. Emphasize the major ideas.
5. Try to make the chart reflect your own insights.

Note the sample chart on page 76.

Example of Horizontal Chart—Book of James

Theme: Living faith is revealed through active works.

Key words: Faith, works, doers.

Key verses: 2:17, 26. "Faith apart from works is dead."

Perfection of Faith	Proof of Faith	Practical Evidences of Faith		Power of Faith
1. Through Trials	2. Through works	3. Through wisdom	4. Through attitudes	5. Through perseverance
1. Salutation. (1) 2. Possibilities of trials. (2-11) Purpose (2-4) Guidance (5-8) Strength (9-11) 3. Possibilities of temptations. (12-18) Source (12-15) Contrast (16-18) 4. Power of the Word. (19-27)	1. Faith demands works. (1-13) 2. Faith worthless without works. (14-17) 3. Works the proof of faith. (18-26) Examples: Abraham Rahab	1. Faith expressed through right use of tongue. (1-12) Possibilities Characteristics 2. Faith expressed through wisdom. (13-18)	1. Faith expressed through right attitudes. (1-12) toward world toward God toward neighbor 2. Faith expressed through reliance on God. (13-17)	1. Patient in suffering. (1-11) 2. Honest in speech. (12) 3. Persevering in prayer. (13-20)

Characteristics of Book of James:

Practical rather than doctrinal.

Emphasis on moral and social living.

Many exhortations.

Lessons:

1. Let trials perfect your character.
2. Show your faith in deeds of love.
3. Beware of the uncontrolled tongue.
4. Pray!

Example of Vertical Chart—James 4

Theme: Faith revealed through proper attitudes

Source of Problems	(1-6) Problems—Wars and strife

Reason

    Because of wrong attitudes
      Ruled by evil desires

    Because of wrong relationships
      Friendship with world
      Enmity with God |
	(7-10)
	(11-12)
	(13-17)

Practice A — Make a Vertical Chart of James 4

Read James 4 and make a summary vertical chart of the contents of the chapter. On page 77 there is the beginning of the chart. Complete the chart by summarizing the content of each section with some concise statements. In the left margin, place a summary title for each section. If there are several in a group, you might divide the paragraphs and each work on one. Then make a composite chart.

Practice B — Focus on Smaller Section

(Select the one you have time to do.)

1. Thorough study of one paragraph

Select one paragraph and make a thorough study of it as you have done in previous chapters.

a) Use observation form:

Observations	Diagram of passage	Questions for Understanding

b) Select a few key questions for interpretation.

c) Share how one of the key ideas in this passage might be applied and actualized in your life.

2. Short study

Select one of the key verses or set of verses and use the following form for consideration of these verses.

Verses	Interpretation	Actualization
Observations about the verses	Insights gained through defining words, comparing translations, looking at one cross-reference.	Ways I can actualize the truths of these verses in my life:

Practice C – Personalize Biblical Teachings

As you reflect on ways to apply and actualize some of the statements in this chapter, consider some of the following suggestions.

1. Discuss the following statement.

"Desire is the root of all the evils which ruin and divide men."
Do you agree or disagree? Why?

2. Study the key exhortations in James 4:7-10.

Is there any significance in the order of them? How would you carry out some of these exhortations? Give illustrations.

3. Read James 4 prayerfully.

As you read ask yourself these questions:
   a) What special area in my life is the Lord speaking to me personally in this chapter?
   b) What are some prayers of thanksgiving, confession, petition, intercession for me to pray?

For some time you have been studying this letter of James. You have been involved in learning skills in observing, asking questions, interpreting, diagramming, charting, summarizing, analyzing, applying. All Bible skills are a means to an end: to discover the message God has in his Word for each one of us and to actualize the teachings in our lives. James' purpose for writing this letter was not to prove whether a man is saved by faith or works, but to reveal that faith and works are inseparable.

Now that you are coming to the close of your study, you need to say to yourself: "What has the Lord been revealing to me personally through the study in James? What are the evidences that my faith is a living faith revealed through the fruit and works in my life?"

This is your final Discovery Skills Practice. There are several suggestions given for you to do, relating to James 5 and the entire book. Select one or more from each list.

Practice A — Study James 5

1. Make a horizontal chart of James 5.

Title each paragraph and list the important ideas in each paragraph.

2. Read James 5 prayerfully.

Spend some time meditating on one aspect in the chapter. Express your thoughts in some devotional way—in a song, a poem, a prayer or devotional thought.

3. Make a special study of James 5:13-16

Key observations	Interpretation of some of the key ideas	One way I can actualize the teachings in this passage

Practice B — Review the Book of James

1. Make a chart.

Make a horizontal or vertical chart or summary diagram reflecting the main teachings in the letter of James.

On page 76 there is a chart showing some of the general teachings in the book. Let your chart or diagram reflect what you consider the most important teachings in the book for you personally.

2. Study a theme.

Select one of the themes in James (suffering, temptations, tongue, prayer, faith and works) and make a special study, reflecting observations, interpretation and application.

3. Team project.

Team up with one other person and together plan some way to involve the rest of the persons in your study group or class to consider some aspect or teaching in James.

a) Select some hymn for them to sing which reflects a teaching in James.

b) Write words to a familiar tune or compose music for one of the passages in James for the others to sing.

c) Present some imaginary conversation with James on an issue.

d) Provide some open-ended or true-and-false statements for your classmates to consider.

e) Have your classmates apply some teaching in James to present-day problems through the use of newspaper clippings, pictures, cartoons, or advertisements.

Practice C – Evaluation

1. Some teachings in James which have strengthened my faith are . . .
2. One way in which the study of James has changed my attitudes or actions . . .
3. Some of the study skills which I have found most helpful are . . .
4. Some of the frustrations I had are . . .
5. Ways I have already used the skills or can use them are . . .

CHAPTER 12

Studying a Longer Book

So far in our studies we have worked with shorter passages of Scripture in order to learn skills in Bible study. The primary purpose of the skills is to teach you how to think when studying Scripture. Whether you are studying a paragraph or a whole book, the basic approach to the study is the same. Let us review the general procedures.

OBSERVE   . . . exactly what the writer is saying.

INTERPRET . . . carefully what the author has written so as to gain insight into the meanings.

SUMMARIZE . . . concisely so as to set forth the major teachings in the passage, chapter, or book.

EVALUATE   . . . fairly so as to determine the relevance of the biblical teachings to present-day living.

APPLY   . . . personally in order to make the biblical teachings meaningful in your own life.

ACTUALIZE . . . your convictions. Put into action the challenges you find in your study.

Whether you are studying a verse, a paragraph, a chapter, or a book, the principal steps in the process are the same. They are basic in all study processes, but the manner in which you apply the steps will be determined by the amount of material to cover, the purpose of your study and the time you have for study. We know that a person who does a great deal of Bible study and teaching has to develop short cuts. We never minimize the importance of thorough study, but you will find that the more skilled you become in learning how to study, the more you can accomplish in a shorter time.

Procedure in the Study of a Gospel

Let us imagine that you are to teach one of the Gospels in a Sunday Bible class. The following procedure may help you in your preparation for the class. We shall use the book of Mark for our illustrations. The same procedure could be followed if you were studying the book of Acts or one of the Old Testament historical books. Your procedure for study would also be a procedure for teaching the book.

STEP ONE: Observe the Whole Book

1. Skim through the book of Mark quickly to obtain a general idea of the content.

2. Read the whole book more carefully with one purpose in mind: to observe the general content and grouping of material.

3. As you read the Gospel the second time, work out a rough horizontal chart, blocking out 16 spaces across your sheet, one space for each chapter in the book of Mark. Number the spaces up to 16. As you read each chapter, summarize its content in a brief phrase or title and write this in your chapter space.

The Gospels are divided into sections, such as, early life of Jesus, early ministry, later ministry, general discourses (sermons and parables), Jesus' passion and resurrection. As you read, note the relationship of the chapters to each other. Block together those which have to do with the specific phases of Jesus' life, such as his preparation, ministry, sufferings and death, resurrection. When you have finished reading the book, you should have before you a graphic summary of the whole book, showing general chapter content and the main structure of the book.

STEP TWO: Observe the Chapters

The second step is to study carefully the individual chapters. Again, it is very helpful to block out the material in chart form. Sketch a horizontal chart for each chapter and allow as many spaces as there are paragraphs. Title your paragraphs by summarizing the main thought of each paragraph into a short phrase. Study the paragraphs to see which are on the same topic. Block these together as a division. Note how the paragraphs are tied together and their relationship to each other. In the study of each chapter there are many features which you can record on your chart.

1. Make note of key persons, places, events, key ideas, characteristics of people, the actions of people, their reactions and attitudes.

2. Keep in mind the patterns of literary structure as described in Chapter 4. Make note of significant repetitions, comparisons, contrasts, centers of interest, progressions of ideas, climax. Note whether there

are contrasts, repetition of ideas or progression of ideas between paragraphs.

3. Note how the message of the portion is emphasized: through a parable? narrative? question? quotations? story? conversation?

4. Note the atmosphere. How would you describe it? controversial? tense? challenging? peaceful?

5. Study the reaction of the persons to each other and to Jesus. Especially note those who oppose him, reasons for opposition, and methods used against him.

6. Make a special study of the miracles of Jesus and of his discourses.

7. Discover what the chapter teaches about the four main concepts of the Bible: God, man, sin, redemption.

8. Observe the human touches in the Gospel narratives. Make note of those incidents which seem true to life. Note in what ways the biblical characters act and react as normal human beings.

STEP THREE: Study Background

In the study of a historical book like a Gospel, it is important that you understand the geographical and historical background of the material recorded. Consult a Bible dictionary or encyclopedia for descriptions of such persons as Pharisees and Sadducees, and for historical figures such as King Herod or Pontius Pilate. Locate on a map the events in the life of Jesus. You will find it very helpful to make your own map and indicate the location of the events in his life.

STEP FOUR: Interpret

Although in the study of a longer book you may not record your interpretive questions as you did in your study of the Epistle of James, you should continually ask yourself questions: Why is this event recorded? Why does Jesus do what he does? What is the meaning, significance and implication of his statements, sermons, parables, stories? Why do people act and react as they do? Why is so much space given to some events and so little to others? What is the purpose of the author recording what he does? Why did he not record what some of the other Gospel writers included? As you chart the chapters and study individual paragraphs, write down some of your key interpretive questions.

When interpreting narrative passages, it is very important to try to recreate in your own mind the historical situation. Attempt to imagine how you would have felt, acted, reacted if you had witnessed the scene recorded. For example, try to recreate the thoughts and emotions of the disciples at the Transfiguration scene, at the Last Supper, at his crucifixion.

Apply the same steps for interpreting narrative portions as you did with the Epistle of James: pray, meditate, define words, study charac-teristics of people, compare translations, look up cross-references, con-sult other helps. As always, summarize your findings.

STEP FIVE: Summarize

Always think about summarizing what you have been studying. Step One was to read the whole book and work out a rough chart of the book. As you study each chapter more thoroughly, this rough chart should become enlarged to include many insights which you have gained through your study. After a thorough study of a book, you might work out several charts, showing different aspects of the book.

As you summarize a book, note the way the writer has organized his material. It is helpful if you indicate this organization on your chart.

Biographical—in terms of the lives of people.

Historical—in terms of the succession of events.

Chronological—in terms of when events happened.

Geographical—in terms of the places where events happened.

Logical or ideological—in terms of the ideas themselves.

STEP SIX: Study Individual Passages

You may want to make a special study of some of the more important passages, such as the special events in the life of Jesus, his sermons or parables.

If it is a discourse passage such as one of Jesus' sermons, you will find it helpful to diagram it as is suggested in Chapter 8 and make observations and ask yourself questions as you have been doing in your previous studies. Also follow the pattern you have used for inter-preting a passage.

If it is a narrative, follow the suggestions in Chapter 5, Studying a Narrative. Use the words *where, when, who, what, why, how* as your guides for observing details.

STEP SEVEN: Apply, Actualize

Application and actualization of biblical teachings is as important in studying the Gospels as they are in studying the epistles. You should personalize the narratives as well as the exhortations and admonitions in the Gospels. Here are some ways:

WHEN PERSONALIZING DISCOURSE MATERIAL, USE SUCH QUESTIONS AS THESE:

1. What are some truths to believe?

2. What are some promises to claim?

3. What are some attitudes and actions to follow?

4. What are some relationships to consider?

WHEN PERSONALIZING NARRATIVES, FOLLOW THESE SUGGESTIONS:

1. Read the story imaginatively, making the story your own.

2. Identify with one of the characters, one that seems to best reflect your feelings and concerns right now.

3. Determine where you are in terms of the experiences of this character. For instance, if you were to identify yourself with blind Bartimaeus in his story (Mark 10:46-52), decide where you are right now:

    a) sitting blindly by the side of a road;
    b) crying out to Jesus;
    c) hearing Jesus invite you to come to him;
    d) asking for a specific thing from him;
    e) experiencing his power;
    f) rejoicing in your new life.

4. Identify the Good News in the story for yourself.

CHAPTER 13

Personalizing Biblical Teachings

In your study you may have gained skill in observing and in interpreting the truths found in Scripture. It is possible to teach yourself to become a profound intellectual Bible student and yet miss the ultimate purpose of all Bible study: to permit the Word of God to speak in a personal way to your heart. To observe and interpret the facts are only the first two steps in the study. There is little gained unless you apply the truths to your own life in a practical way. In this chapter we shall consider the three aspects of study that have to do with personal appropriation of biblical teachings: *evaluation, application, actualization.*

EVALUATION — What Is the Value of Biblical Teachings?

In studying Scripture, you need to appraise the value of usefulness of a biblical teaching before you can apply it. This does not mean that you set yourself up as a critical judge, but with an honest heart you should continually appraise the general validity of a Bible passage in relation to present-day living. "Does the Bible have value for the persons of today? Does it meet the needs of the people today? How valid is the message of a particular passage? To whom can these truths be applied?"

Suggestions for Evaluating:

The following questions may help you in evaluating a portion of Scripture.

1. WHAT WAS THE PURPOSE OF THE AUTHOR? Did he accomplish his purpose? We should never evaluate the worth of a passage unless we do so with the author's purpose in mind. Otherwise we are unfair to the author. Many people condemn the Bible because they say it is

87

not scientific or historically accurate. Such an accusation is unfair because they have failed to take into consideration the purpose of the writers of the Bible. Their purpose was never to give a historical or scientific account of events, but to proclaim God's message of salvation as revealed through events and persons.

2. FOR WHOM WAS THE BIBLICAL PORTION WRITTEN? In evaluating we should try to understand the setting, time, ethics of that day, the people to whom the book was written, their experiences, customs, and needs. Too often we evaluate a passage through our "twentieth-century" eyes and misinterpret the message.

3. WHAT ARE GENERAL TRUTHS AND WHAT ARE LOCAL TRUTHS? Some passages of Scripture were written for a certain period of history and therefore are local in application. The Bible student must distinguish between local truths applicable for specific periods in history, and general truths which can be applied to any age. Although James wrote his epistle for a definite group of people, the statements he makes are equally applicable today. In the Old Testament we have some statements which we cannot apply to standards of today, but behind every local truth there is usually a universal truth which can be applied in all ages.

4. WHAT IS THE RELATION OF THE TRUTHS FOUND IN A PARTICULAR PASSAGE TO THE WHOLE MESSAGE OF THE BIBLE? No single portion should be evaluated apart from the whole message of the Bible. The basic truths of the Bible are never contradictory when considered in their own context and in relation to the whole Bible message.

5. HOW VALID IS THE TRANSLATION? To judge the validity of a passage a person should read it in its original language. Only then can we receive an accurate concept of the real meaning of some of the difficult portions of Scripture. Since most of us cannot read Greek or Hebrew, we should always compare translations in order to gain as clear a picture as possible of what the author said.

6. HOW OBJECTIVE ARE YOU? Evaluations should always be as objective as possible. Personal prejudices and pet whims should not govern your thinking.

APPLICATION — What Do the Biblical Teachings Mean to Me?

In 2 Timothy 3:16-17 Paul states the general purpose of Bible study: *"All Scripture is inspired by God and is useful for teaching the truth, rebuking error, correcting faults, and giving instruction for right living, so that the man who serves God may be fully qualified and equipped to do every kind of good work"* (TEV). In these words we observe that the real purpose of Bible study is to permit the Word of

God to teach us, to reprove us, to correct us, to train us so that we may be equipped to live godly lives and to serve him in all that we do. Thus we realize that all the Bible study skills which we have been discussing are only a means to this end: that God may accomplish his good work in our lives through his Word. Unless we apply what we have learned, our study has not accomplished its primary purpose, even though we may have gained much intellectual knowledge.

In fact it is very dangerous to study the Bible and not be open to its message. The Word of God is power. It either penetrates hearts or it hardens hearts. The person who is not open to the Holy Spirit as he speaks through the Word can consciously or unconsciously be rejecting the truths and in the process harden his heart. *"Today, when you hear his voice, do not harden your hearts"* Hebrews 3:7-8.

Ways to Apply Biblical Teachings

As you consider how to apply biblical teachings, there are several key questions you might ask yourself to guide you in the process.

1. What am I to believe? One of the outcomes of Bible study has to do with the doctrines and teachings on which we build our faith. As you study a passage you should ask yourself: "What is in this passage that I am to believe—about God, Jesus Christ, Holy Spirit, grace, mercy, sin, forgiveness, hope, eternal life, etc.?"

2. What am I to do? Another outcome of Bible study concerns actions and attitudes. As you study a passage you might ask yourself some of these questions:

ACTIONS: How am I to reveal my faith through my actions? Are there actions which I need to change?

ATTITUDES: What do I learn about positive and negative attitudes? What are the results of each kind? What do I learn about emotions? Is there help suggested for release from destructive emotions such as fear, worry, anxiety, hate, resentment, jealousy?

SIN: What sins are pointed out in my life? Are there some I need to confess to God? to my fellowmen? need to forsake?

3. What do I learn about relationships? While the questions which have already been listed are important, another key question which needs to be considered has to do with relationships. The Bible has primarily to do with relationships. It is a record of God's relationship with man and man's response to this relationship. While the Bible focuses on relationships, the tendency of the church has been to focus on beliefs. As Christians we can all believe that the Bible is the Word of God and yet vary a great deal in what we consider to be the truths in the Bible. One of the reasons we have many denominations is that we disagree in what we are to believe and what we are to do. In fact concern for "right beliefs" has sometimes severed relationships—split families, congregations and even denominations.

Christianity is not so much "believing in the right things" as being involved in the "right relationships." One of the definitions of the term *righteous* is "right relationships." My status as a Christian is based on my personal relationship with Jesus Christ, a relationship God made possible through the redemptive work of Christ. Christianity is also concerned about right relationships with our fellowmen, with God's created world, and with ourselves. We live in a world of broken relationships which Christ came to mend and to heal. If I am rightly related to God through Jesus Christ, this relationship should be reflected in my relationship with others, with the world and with myself—relationships that are loving, caring, helping, unifying, forgiving, healing, freeing.

As you study a passage, consider what it has to say about relationships. Ask yourself the question: What does this passage say to me . . .

- about my relationship with God through Jesus Christ?
- about my relationship with others? in my family? in my community? in my congregation? in the world?
- about my relationship with God's created world?
- about my relationship with myself?

4. What is the Good News for me? This fourth question is probably the most personal of all. When studying a Bible passage, ask yourself, "Is there Good News for me in this passage?" The Bible is the Book of Good News—the Good News of God reconciling us to himself through Jesus Christ while we were yet sinners.

But too often when we study our Bibles, we focus on the "bad news"—the bad news that we are sinners, failures, imperfect persons, never able to measure up to the demands of the Law. Knowing how often we fall short of what we thing we ought to be, we are filled with guilt and make resolutions to do better next time—only to find that next time we fail again.

Gospel means *good news.* Jesus came to proclaim *good news,* demonstrating it through his words, life, death, and resurrection. He came as Savior to free us from all that enslaves and hinders our relationship with him. He came as Healer for our illnesses, sorrows, disappointments, defeats. He came as Reconciler in our broken relationships with God, with others and within ourselves.

The Good News of Christ is that I can approach Bible study as a "loser." I don't have to strive and struggle to meet the requirements of the Law. The message of the Bible is for losers like me who can never make it on their own. The Good News is that I don't have to make it on my own. Christ has done it all for me. I can bring to the foot of the cross all my sins, my guilts, my problems, my defeats, my mistakes and find that Christ is for losers like me. He heals me—frees me—redeems me. To grow in grace means to grow more and more aware of my need of him.

When you study a passage, look for the "Good News" in the passage —the Good News of grace, of forgiveness, of healing, of the reconciling love of God.

ACTUALIZATION—How Do I Personally Actualize Biblical Teachings?

To actualize means to bring into action those insights gained through your study. It is possible to intellectually apply biblical teachings but never really actualize them—make them a reality in your own life. To move from the intellectual assent to concrete reality is the problem which faces us all. Let me suggest some ways.

Meditate on the Teachings

To meditate is to contemplate and ponder some passages in a quiet, unhurried manner. In this day of hurry, fury, and worry, few of us spend much time in prayerful meditation. Too often we do a little bit of reading and a little bit of praying, convinced that we haven't time for more. No wonder God seems so far away and silent. We seldom sit still long enough to give him time to speak to us. If application is to be something other than a superficial giving assent to things we ought to do (but never do them), we need to practice meditation. Here are some things you might do.

- Relax your mind and body. Think of God's Spirit as releasing all your tensions.
- Read slowly and prayerfully a passage. Try reading it aloud sometimes.
- Consider what the passage has to say to you personally, using some of the questions suggested under *ways to apply*.
- Imagine the Lord speaking to you concerning some teaching in the passage.
- Reflect on the passage as a guide for prayer in terms of confession, petition, intercession, thanksgiving and praise.

Express Our Faith in Concrete Ways

There are many general ways in which to express our faith. We can share verbally what Christ means to us in our homes, community, and world. We reflect the sincerity of our faith in our willingness to share our time, money, energy in helping the needy, the lonely, the sick, the aged. A very visible evidence of our faith is shown in our willingness to become involved in church and community action groups in the struggle against poverty, racism, and prejudice. We can verbalize our faith creatively in poems, hymns, letters, and articles—and visualize our concepts in illustrations, drawings, banners, pictures, and construction projects.

Share Convictions and Concerns with Others

If in your Bible study you become concerned about some problem, need, or issue, it is helpful to share this problem or need with others. This is one of the values of studying in a small group. You will find that some of your group members may have the same problem or need. Together you can consider possibilities and encourage each other in potential actions. If your problem is very personal, share it with a special friend, your pastor, or a counselor. If your concern has to do with church or community, your entire group should discuss how to meet it.

Make a Verbal Commitment

Just sharing or discussing an issue or problem is not enough. There is need to make definite decisions and verbal commitments. Unless we verbalize our feelings and decisions, we have difficulty appropriating what the Lord has for us. This is the reason that leaders in evangelistic meetings challenge persons to make a decision for Christ and openly give witness to the decision. Many a person has been helped to appropriate God's love and forgiveness by making a verbal commitment to Christ in the presence of one or two persons. So it is with any problem or need you face. After discussing it with others, if you make a verbal commitment concerning it, you will find greater strength and courage to carry out your plans relating to it.

Pray with One Another

Prayer is a very important aspect of the doing. Most of us need the help, power, guidance, and strength of the Lord. While we need to pray individually about our decisions, we need the prayers of others as well. Praying with others seems to lift burdens and provides additional strength for carrying out decisions.

CHAPTER **14**

Discovering with Others

Maybe you are asking the questions, "Why study the Bible with others? Isn't it enough just to study the Bible by ourselves?" Emil Brunner, a leading theologian, has said: "Faith grows out of fellowship. We need others to be able to believe. One cannot be a Christian by oneself. All sorts of things can be done alone, but one cannot be a Christian by oneself. My own weak faith must constantly be awakened, strengthened, purified by the faith of others. We must come together to believe. 'Where two or three are gathered in my name, there I am in the midst of them.'"

We Need Each Other

While it is true we come together on Sunday morning for worship, this is mainly an individual experience. We need also to meet in small groups to help each other grow in our Christian faith. The church is a fellowship of believers. The term fellowship implies a close relationship with others, a sense of belonging, a caring for one another, a bearing of each other's burdens. A small-group Bible study is one of the places in which these things can happen. It can be a place where we share with each other what the Bible is saying to us, share our concerns, doubts, fears, and questions. It is a time when we can encourage, strengthen, and support one another, pray for and with one another. Faith grows more deeply in such a fellowship. Countless persons are yearning and hungry for such a fellowship.

Our Role in a Group

As members of a Bible study group, there are at least four ways we can view ourselves in terms of our role in the group.

As a Receiver

We can attend a Bible study group as a *receiver*. We may or may not have done much studying before the meeting, but our primary purpose for attending the meeting is to receive. We hope to receive something from the leader and possibly from other members in the group. This has been the traditional role for many persons involved in Bible studies. They view themselves mainly as receivers—either because they feel they have very little to give or because their leader does all of the talking and they are not expected to give anything. As receivers, we measure the success of the Bible study by what we received, disappointed or inspired, depending on the effectiveness of the leader.

As a Giver

Or we may view our role as a *giver* at a Bible study. This is the role assumed by many leaders of Bible classes. Most of them invest much time in study before the meeting and come prepared to give. They view the members of their group as receivers. One of the problems of this role is that the burden of the study rests on the shoulders of the giver. If as a leader we are not very well prepared or are inadequate, some of our *receivers* may become disappointed and quit our class. The entire responsibility for the success of the study rests on our ability to give.

As Receiver-Giver

We may view our role as *receiver-giver*. This means that we will study before the meeting and come prepared to both give and receive from the others. This can be our attitude even though we are the leader. We come hoping to involve our group members in discussion so that we can give and receive from one another.

As An Enabler

The fourth kind of role we may assume in a group is that of an *enabler*. The difference between this role and the other roles is that in the first three roles our concern mainly centers in ourself. In the role of the *enabler* our concern also centers in the members of our group. Traditionally, our attitude in terms of Bible studies has been somewhat selfish. Even though we view our role as *receiver-giver,* our focus is still mainly on ourselves—what we can receive or give at a Bible study. Even as the leader, our reaction often centers in self. Our happiness or disappointment is affected by what we feel we were able to give or receive from the other members.

If we view ourselves as enablers, our concern will also include our group members and what is happening to them. To enable means to call forth, to allow to emerge, to help someone else realize his potentials. To be an enabler means to call forth the best in each member of the group, to enable him to share his ideas, his hopes, his concerns, to help him realize his potentials as both a receiver and giver. An enabler is one who blesses us and helps us be a blessing.

Why Become Enablers?

Maybe you are asking, "Why become enablers? Is it not enough for a study just to center on the message in the Bible? Why this emphasis on group relationships?" We need each other to grow in our Christian faith. A Bible study to have its greatest impact should have two dimensions: the vertical in terms of our relationship to God, and the horizontal in terms of our relationship with others. The most immediate effect in terms of others should be with those in our own group.

Countless persons have attended Bible studies, burdened with problems and guilt, feeling lonely and discouraged. They have listened to some inspiring studies, but have gone home feeling just as lonely and discouraged. The message contained hope for them, but they were unable to appropriate the message and make it their own. Most of us are so constituted that unless we can express our feelings, our doubts, our fears, our questions, we have difficulty personalizing God's message of hope, love, grace, and mercy. Even though there are opportunities for discussion, unless we feel safe in the group, we will not share our true feelings; we will just discuss the facts of the Bible.

Most of us have a poor self-image. We do not really know our own potential. Someone has said that most people realize about ten percent of their potential. Ninety percent lies hidden beneath a pile of failures, unhappy memories, fears, and guilt feelings. There is a wide gap between what we think we ought to be and what we think we are. We feel depressed and guilty about the gap.

Therefore, many of us view ourselves only as receivers. We feel that we do not have much to give. Most of us hide behind masks, fearful of letting others know our true selves. We refuse leadership roles and hesitate to share our ideas, feeling that what we have to say "is not of much value." We become *enablers* when we are willing to take off our masks and share with others our thoughts, our fears, our doubts, our hang-ups. When we do this, we find that others have the same problems we do.

As enablers we seek to establish a climate of trust, acceptance, and understanding in which all can feel free to share hopes and dreams, doubts and fears. Many of us have experienced what an enabling group can do for us. We have fearfully and hesitantly accepted an office or agreed to lead a Bible study. Our group members have encouraged and supported us. We gained a new concept of the gifts which the Lord has given us. We were enabled to realize our potentials. By ourselves we cannot develop a positive self-image. We need the affirmation of others to help us think new thoughts about ourselves, to identify and help us realize our potentials.

How to Become Enablers

UNDERSTAND THAT MOST OF US ARE ALIKE. While we all have different backgrounds and problems, in some ways we are very much alike:

— are afraid to make mistakes and reveal ignorance
— fear the disapproval of others

— worry about what people will think of us
— have little confidence in ourselves as students
— fear sharing ideas because we think they might be wrong
— feel guilty about many things
— avoid situations wherein we might be embarrassed
— are slow to accept new ideas

BE CONCERNED ABOUT EACH OTHER'S PERSONAL GROWTH. The very way we treat each other in our group will create an enabling climate in which all can grow.

— Encourage each other to share feelings as well as ideas.
— Listen carefully to one another's contributions and add to them.
— Be careful never to dominate a discussion.
— Be open and honest in sharing doubts, fears, frustrations, as well as hopes and dreams.
— Respect one another's ideas even though they differ from ours.
— Allow one another the right to his opinion without judgment.
— Encourage those who are hesitant about sharing.
— Identify with the problems of others.

EXPRESS OUR CONCERN FOR EACH OTHER IN CONCRETE WAYS. We reflect our concern for each other by the concrete things we do.

— Study for our group meeting, especially if we have accepted the responsibility for some special assignment.
— Be faithful in attendance. If we cannot attend, let our group know.
— Affirm, encourage and support each other in what is said and done.
— Try to help one another identify each one's gifts.
— Be on the alert for the lonely, the troubled, the needy.
— Be sensitive to the feelings of others.
— Pray for and with one another.

My Prayer

As I come to the end of the book, I would like to share with you my prayer that through these suggestions you have discovered . . .

• the joys of studying the Bible in a systematic way;
• the value of studying and sharing together with others;
• the power of the Holy Spirit to guide you in your study;
• the reality of the love and grace of Jesus Christ
• the potentials and gifts which the Lord has given you and ways you can use them in his ministry;
• new insights in how to develop more satisfying relationships with others;
• greater concern for the needs of others;
• greater freedom, peace and joy in your personal life as you learn to live in the grace and forgiveness of Jesus Christ.